THE UNOFFICIAL HUNGER GAMES COOKBOOK

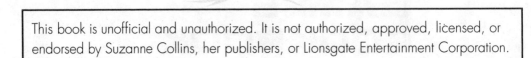

THE UNOFFICIAL HUNGER GAMES COOKBOOK

From Lamb Stew to "Groosling"—
More Than 150 Recipes Inspired by
The Hunger Games Trilogy

EMILY ANSARA BAINES

AdamsmeDia
AVON, MASSACHUSETTS

Published by
Adams Media, a division of F+W Media, Inc.
57 Littlefield Street, Avon, MA 02322. U.S.A.
www.adamsmedia.com

ISBN 10: 1-4405-2658-3
ISBN 13: 978-1-4405-2658-9
eISBN 10: 1-4405-2962-0
eISBN 13: 978-1-4405-2962-7

Contains material adapted and abridged from: *The Everything® Wild Game Cookbook*, by
Karen Eagle, copyright © 2006 by F+W Media, Inc., ISBN 10: 1-5933-7545-X, ISBN 13:
978-1-5933-7545-4; and *The Everything® Guide to Foraging*, by Vickie Shuffer, copyright
© 2011 by F+W Media, Inc., ISBN 10: 1-4405-1276-0, ISBN 13: 978-1-4405-1276-6.

Printed by RR Donnelley, Harrisonburg, VA, USA.

10 9 8 7 6 5 4 3 2 1

October 2011

Library of Congress Cataloging-in-Publication Data
is available from the publisher.

This publication is designed to provide accurate and authoritative information with regard to
the subject matter covered. It is sold with the understanding that the publisher is not engaged
in rendering legal, accounting, or other professional advice. If legal advice or other expert
assistance is required, the services of a competent professional person should be sought.

—From a *Declaration of Principles* jointly adopted by a Committee of the
American Bar Association and a Committee of Publishers and Associations

This book is unofficial and unauthorized. It is not authorized, approved, licensed, or endorsed
by Suzanne Collins, her publishers, or Lionsgate Entertainment Corporation. "Hunger Games"
is a registered trademark of Suzanne Collins.

This book is available at quantity discounts for bulk purchases.
For information, please call 1-800-289-0963.

For Keagan

CONTENTS

Chapter 4:
Humble Beginnings >> 81

INTRODUCTION

There's never a dull moment in the Hunger Games universe. And yet, all of the exciting (albeit terrifying) experiences that the characters face pale in comparison to the vital, yet elemental, role that food plays throughout the series. Here, food is so much more than just something to eat. Instead, it represents a variety of conflicts that the characters, regardless of background, must struggle against. Food represents the ever-widening gap between the haves (those in the Capitol) and the have-nots (almost everyone else). It gives the characters strength both by nurturing their physical bodies and reminding them of their emotional roots. The characters use food as a form of power; food can be used to uplift those in need, while its absence can push those in need further down. Food is also representative of survival; those who are self-sufficient enough to find food live, those who don't, die.

Yet food isn't just a basic necessity for survival, it's also a form of communication when all other forms have been denied.

During Katniss's first Hunger Games, Haymitch communicates with her using bread. This sly form of messaging is replicated in the Quarter Quell, allowing Finnick to learn the hour of their rescue.

And for Katniss, food isn't just a form of communication, it's a form of identity. After all, her father named her for the nutritious root, noting, "As long as you can find yourself, you'll never starve" (*The Hunger Games*, Chapter 4). And in *Mockingjay*, we learn that Panem, Katniss's country—and oftentimes, enemy—literally means *bread*. Plutarch, the Head Gamemaker, explains to Katniss that Panem's name is a reference to an ancient saying about Rome, *Panem et Circenses*, which translates into "Bread and Circuses." The Romans, like the citizens of Panem, gave up their right to fair political representation in return for full stomachs and plenty of entertainment. An unwise choice that later cost them not only their rights, but their civilization. When you think about the relationship the Capitol holds with its districts, and the ultimate entertainment of the Hunger Games, it's easy to realize along with Katniss that the description holds not just for Rome, but for the Capitol. This connection to Rome foreshadows what will occur at the end of the series: Like Rome, the Capitol must fall.

As you cook your way through *The Hunger Games*, you'll notice that there are two distinct types of recipes. First, there are the decadent dishes that helped contribute to the overindulged attitudes of the Capitol's bourgeoisie and lulled those citizens into a false sense of security and entitlement—until Katniss and the Districts rose up against them. Whether it's the lamb stew with dried plums that Katniss adores, the rich cakes Peeta so admires, or a variety of game drizzled with luxuriously sweet and savory sauces, these recipes are sure to fill you up, if not put you in a sugar coma.

The other, less well-known, recipes that you'll find throughout represent the difficult lives of the inhabitants of the Districts. As those in the Capitol gorge on elegant cooked delicacies, Katniss and her peers scrape by on a mixture of nuts, berries, wild game, and bread. These citizens know not only how to hunt and forage, but cook their own food with only the most meager of materials. These actions show off their survival instincts and foreshadow the outcome of the rebellion. Even when Katniss is in the Capitol-controlled arena

during the Hunger Games, she's able to keep both herself and her allies alive by her resourceful knowledge of edible plants and hunting.

Thus, this cookbook serves as a portal into Katniss's two worlds—one of luxury and pampering, and one of hardship and labor. Regardless of which world you choose to cook from, the recipes in this cookbook are a fun and delicious way for you and your family to transport yourselves alongside Katniss, Peeta, and Gale while they fight for their freedom—and the right to a full stomach. Enjoy!

CHAPTER 1

BREAKFAST OF CHAMPIONS

The motto "breakfast is the most important meal of the day" is one lesson you likely learned at a very young age. Thus, it comes as no surprise that the Capitol, District 12, and even the infamous District 13 all possess a wealth of recipes for this very important meal. After all, without a nutritious breakfast, how can the workers of the Seam or even the socialites of the Capitol expect to have the energy to greet their very busy—albeit very different—days? In this chapter you'll find a wide range of breakfast recipes, so whether you're craving the Capitol's Outrageous Orange Muffins with Sweet Preserves or Mrs. Everdeen's Breakfast of Mush, you're sure to find something both filling and delicious to start your own successful day.

1

HEARTY HAM AND EGG TART

When an assortment of eggs and ham are made available to Katniss, Peeta, and the rest of their crew on the train on the way to the Capitol, it's easy to see the juxtaposition between the extreme poverty the characters have faced and the luxuries those in the Capitol enjoy. This recipe easily utilizes these foods into one delicious dish that is both savory and sweet. If you're a fan of cheese and quiche you'll find yourself enjoying this breakfast tart almost as much as Peeta and Katniss!
(*The Hunger Games*, Chapter 4)

Yields 1 tart

> Crust:

2 tablespoons ice water

2 tablespoons chilled whipping cream

1 tablespoon vanilla extract

1 ½ cups all-purpose flour

1 teaspoon coarse kosher salt

1 teaspoon baking powder

1 ¼ cups (2 ½ sticks) cold unsalted butter, cut into pieces

> Filling:

½ cup chopped onion

¼ cup chopped green bell pepper

1 tablespoon butter

1 ½ cups fully cooked ham, cubed or shredded

6 eggs

½ cup milk

¼ cup heavy cream

½ teaspoon salt

½ teaspoon pepper

1 cup shredded Cheddar cheese

½ cup grated fresh Parmesan cheese

1. Combine ice water, chilled whipping cream, and vanilla extract. Set aside.

2. In a large bowl, combine flour, salt, and baking powder. Scatter butter pieces over dry ingredients. Using your fingertips, quickly pinch butter with flour mixture until butter is coarsely mixed in (you'll have pieces of dough in varying small sizes; you should aim for the size of peas).

3. Add the ice water and cream mixture to dough. Mix in with hands or a wooden spoon until moist clumps form. Add more ice water if dough is still too dry. Gather dough into a ball; flatten into a disk. Wrap in plastic;

chill for at least one hour. Let soften slightly at room temperature before rolling out into tart pan.

4. Butter a 9" tart or springform pan with a removable bottom. Place softened dough in middle of pan and, using floured fingertips, spread out evenly across the bottom and up the sides of the tart pan, pressing lightly with your fingertips to ensure an even crust. Use your thumbs to press dough to the side of the pan. Make sure the dough on the side of the pan is evenly thick (otherwise you will have uneven baking).

5. Preheat oven to 375°F.

6. In a skillet, sauté onion and bell peppers in butter until tender and slightly browned. Add ham and let sit for five minutes, stirring occasionally. Remove from heat; pour evenly over dough in pan.

7. In a bowl, beat eggs, milk, cream, salt, and pepper. Stir in Cheddar cheese. Pour evenly over ham mixture. Be wary of overflow.

8. Sprinkle Parmesan cheese over top of tart. Bake at 375°F for 30 minutes or until knife inserted comes out clean.

Tips from Your Sponsor

In a time crunch? Never fear! You can skip Steps 1 through 3 by using a premade tart shell or, for a more buttery and flaky crust, use one 8-ounce package of refrigerated crescent rolls. Unroll the crescent roll dough into one long rectangle and press into the tart pan. You will likely have to patchwork the dough into the pan, so be sure to seal seams and perforations before adding filling.

FEARFULLY FRIED POTATOES

While most things related to the Capitol focus on opulence, this simple recipe yields a rich flavor, which makes it a great dish to help Katniss and Peeta transition from life in District 12 to the Capitol. This first breakfast is served on the train as it winds its way to the Capitol, an image that reinforces the idea of transition this recipe imparts.
(*The Hunger Games*, Chapter 4)

Yields 3 servings

2 tablespoons extra-virgin olive oil

½ cups cooked onion, diced

3 cups potatoes, peeled and boiled

Salt and pepper to taste

1. Heat olive oil in a large cast-iron skillet. Sauté onions until they are translucent. Add potatoes and cook until golden brown and warmed through.

2. Season with salt and pepper and serve.

Tips from Your Sponsor

While it's not necessary to fry your potatoes in a cast-iron skillet, it's recommended that you do so. A cast-iron skillet is an excellent addition to any kitchen. Its ability to withstand high heat and its excellent heat diffusion and retention make it a perfect choice for searing, frying, and braising.

HOT AND CRISPY HASH BROWNS

The Capitol is all about superficial change: people's appearances change frequently, outfits change, and the decadent dishes that they eat change often as well. It's quite likely that when Katniss and Peeta are given breakfast, there are a variety of potato options from which they can choose. While not the healthiest dish, this recipe makes for a hot and crispy meal that would make even the poised Effie Trinket loose her cool!
(*The Hunger Games*, Chapter 4)

Yields 4 servings

1 pound baking potatoes, shredded

¼ cup green onions, chopped

¼ cup all-purpose flour

¼ teaspoon cayenne pepper

1 large egg

1 cup vegetable oil (for frying)

Kosher salt and grated black pepper to taste

Hot sauce to taste

Tips from Your Sponsor

Not enough meat in this dish? Add bacon! Before preparing the potatoes, fry eight strips of bacon in a medium skillet until crispy. Then, crumble into tiny pieces and add to potato mixture before cooking.

1. Rinse shredded potatoes, then drain and squeeze or pat dry until all the moisture is out of the potatoes. Place shreds in medium bowl. Mix in onion, flour, cayenne pepper, and egg until evenly distributed.

2. Heat oil in large frying pan over medium heat. When oil sizzles, add potato mixture until it evenly coats entire pan. Let cook without stirring for 5 minutes or until bottom is brown, then flip and cook for an additional 5 minutes. Can be cut into more easily controlled pieces if wanted.

3. Remove from pan; drain on paper towels. Season to taste with salt, pepper, and hot sauce.

ORANGE MUFFINS WITH SWEET PRESERVES

No decadent breakfast at the Capitol would be complete without some options for those who wake up with a roaring sweet tooth! At this point Katniss does not seem all too impressed with the battercakes and their thick orange preserves, which, when you consider that she'd barely even tasted an orange when she arrived in the Capitol, tells us that she's slowly becoming jaded by the lifestyle she's forced to lead when living in the lap of luxury. While Katniss might dislike her sumptuous surroundings now, she'll definitely miss them when fending for herself in the arena.
(*The Hunger Games*, Chapter 4)

Yields 12 muffins and 3 cups preserves

> Muffins:

2 cups all-purpose flour

¼ teaspoon baking soda

2 teaspoons baking powder

1 teaspoon salt

½ cup white sugar

½ cup light brown sugar

2/3 cup orange juice

1 cup (2 sticks) melted butter

2 eggs

1 tablespoon melted butter

¼ cup dark brown sugar

1 teaspoon ground cinnamon

1 teaspoon vanilla extract

> Preserves:

1 cup orange juice

¾ cup white sugar

2½ cups orange marmalade

½ teaspoon ground cloves

½ teaspoon pumpkin pie spice

1. Preheat oven to 350°F. Lightly oil a muffin pan containing 12 regular-sized muffin cups.

2. Combine flour, baking soda, baking powder, salt, and both sugars in a large bowl. Stir in orange juice, 1 cup melted butter, and eggs.

3. Pour batter into 12 muffin cups.

4. Blend the 1 tablespoon melted butter, dark brown sugar, ground cinnamon, and vanilla extract. Sprinkle on top of each muffin. Bake in oven at 350°F for 25 minutes or until inserted toothpick comes out clean.

5. Meanwhile, for preserves, stir juice and sugar in medium saucepan over medium heat until sugar dissolves. Add marmalade, cloves, and pumpkin pie spice; bring to boil. Reduce heat back to medium for 5 minutes and then simmer on low until mixture is reduced to 3 cups, stirring occasionally for about 20 minutes. Cool. If storing, cover and chill in refrigerator. Best if made a day ahead.

Tips from Your Sponsor

This is a relatively unusual preserves recipe, as most such recipes involve taking the actual fruit (chopped or mashed), boiling it with sugar and water, and allowing the mixture to stand for *at least* eight hours. Though time consuming, on cold winter holidays such recipes might be fun to try! If you don't have a local Greasy Sae to go to for possible preserve-making methods, grandmothers are often a wealth of knowledge when it comes to cooking!

FRUIT FRENZY

This fruit salad, placed by Capitol chefs on a bed of ice to keep it chilled—another luxury those starving in the Seam don't have—can be made with a variety of fruit. This berry-heavy fruit recipe is loaded with antioxidants, and is perfect for serving in early summer when fresh berries are abundant. (*The Hunger Games*, Chapter 4)

Yields 4–6 servings of salad

1 cup fresh blueberries

2 cups fresh strawberries

1 cup fresh blackberries

2 cups chopped fresh pineapple

Fresh mint leaves (optional)

1. Using a strainer, gently wash strawberries, blueberries, and then blackberries.

2. Cut stems off of strawberries. Mix all fruit together in a large bowl.

3. Serve alone or with yogurt. Garnish with mint leaves.

Tips from Your Sponsor

While a lot of fruit salad recipes use added sugar, these berries are sweet enough without. Also, if you're tempted to use cantaloupe or any other sort of melon-type fruit, recognize that its soft texture causes a taste runoff that can overcome the overall taste of the dish.

A SUMPTUOUS SAUSAGE SUNRISE

Breakfast in the Capitol means a virtual cornucopia of sweet and savory options, including an assortment of delicious and tender meats that can be easily eaten. The ease with which food is now available stands in sharp contrast to the hunting Katniss usually has to do to get some protein. This sausage recipe, enjoyed by both Katniss and Peeta, employs diverse spices to give a unique edge to an otherwise bland breakfast staple.
***(The Hunger Games**, Chapter 7)*

Yields 5 servings

2 teaspoons dried sage

2 teaspoons salt

1½ teaspoons ground black pepper

½ teaspoon dried marjoram

1½ tablespoons brown sugar

¼ teaspoon crushed red pepper flakes

1 pinch ground cloves

2 pounds ground pork*

Note: If using lean ground pork, you must be extra careful that it does not burn during frying.

Tips from Your Sponsor

For a more heart-healthy option, use 1 pound ground pork and 1 pound fresh ground turkey instead of the 2 pounds pork. This will cut the fat content of your sausage while maintaining the delicious taste!

1. In a small bowl, combine sage, salt, ground black pepper, marjoram, brown sugar, crushed red pepper flakes, and cloves.

2. Place the pork in a large bowl and add the combined spices. Using your hands, thoroughly mix the spices into the pork. Form into patties.

3. Place patties into a large, well-oiled skillet over medium-high heat. Fry for 5 minutes per side, until pork is no longer pink. Let cool for 1 minute, then serve.

SINFUL CINNAMON BUNS

When we first see these Sinful Cinnamon Buns, Peeta is dipping his in chocolate on the train to the Capitol. Later on, after she learns about Peeta's past, Katniss does the same. The same action performed by both tributes illustrates how the two are slowly starting to act in unison and become a team. (*The Hunger Games*, Chapters 4 and 7)

Yields 10 large or 15 medium-sized buns

1 teaspoon white sugar

1 (.25-ounce) package active dry yeast

½ cup warm water

½ cup milk

¼ cup white sugar

¼ cup (½ stick) butter

1 teaspoon salt

2 eggs, beaten

4 cups all-purpose flour

2 tablespoons ground cinnamon

1¼ cups brown sugar

1¼ cups (2½ sticks) butter

¼ cup (½ stick) softened butter

1. In a small bowl, dissolve 1 teaspoon sugar and the yeast in the warm (but not hot) water. Let stand about 10 minutes. It should reach a creamy consistency.

2. Warm the milk in a small saucepan until the milk bubbles; remove from heat. Mix in ¼ cup sugar, ¼ cup butter, and salt. Stir until melted. Let cool.

3. In a large bowl, combine the yeast mixture, milk mixture, eggs, and 1½ cups flour. Using a wooden spoon, stir until thoroughly combined. Add remaining flour ½ cup at a time, beating well after each addition. When the dough has pulled together, turn it out onto a lightly floured surface and knead until smooth and elastic, about 8–10 minutes.

4. Lightly oil a large bowl, place the dough in the bowl, and turn to coat with oil. Cover with a damp cloth and let rise in a warm place until doubled in volume, about 1 hour.

5. In a small mixing bowl, combine cinnamon and brown sugar. Set aside.

6. While dough is rising, melt 1¼ cups butter in a small saucepan over low heat. Stir in 1 cup of the sugar mixture, whisking until smooth. Pour into greased 9" x 13" baking pan.

7. Turn dough out onto a lightly floured surface. Roll into an 18" x 14" rectangle. Brush with 2 tablespoons of the softened butter, leaving a ½" border uncovered; sprinkle with sugar-cinnamon mixture.

8. Starting at long side, tightly roll up, pinching seam to seal. Brush with remaining softened butter. With serrated knife, cut into 10–15 pieces; place cut side down in prepared pan. Cover and let rise for at least 1 hour or until doubled in volume.

9. Preheat oven to 375°F.

10. Bake in preheated oven for 30 minutes, until golden brown. Let cool in pan for 10 minutes, then invert onto serving platter. Scrape remaining filling from the pan onto the rolls.

Tips from Your Sponsor

If you find cutting the buns with a serrated knife difficult, try dental floss! Take a piece of floss, place it across the bread, and pull down on both sides. Presto—a cut piece of dough with no sticky knife to clean up!

CHEESE SOUFFLÉ FOR THE SPOILED SNACKERS

Soufflé need not remain a dessert dish. This cheese soufflé—just rich enough to be worthy of the Capitol—makes for the kind of lavish breakfast with which Katniss might become well-acquainted in the Capitol.
(*The Hunger Games,* Chapter 4)

Yields 8–10 servings

½ cup (1 stick) unsalted butter

½ cup all-purpose flour

22/3 cups whole milk

1 teaspoon kosher salt

½ teaspoon ground white pepper

6 large eggs

3 cups hard cheese (Parmesan, Romano, or Asiago), grated

¼ cup fresh mixed herbs such as parsley, chives, tarragon, or thyme, chopped

Tips from Your Sponsor

Many vegetable dishes can be turned into soufflés with the addition of a white sauce (butter, flour, and milk) along with some eggs. Try adding 1 cup of creamed spinach to this recipe for a spinach soufflé. Or serve this for brunch and add some crumbled bacon!

1. Preheat oven to 400°F. Butter a 2-quart baking dish and set aside.

2. Melt butter in a saucepan and whisk in flour to form a paste. Add ½ cup of the milk and whisk thoroughly to blend. Add the remaining milk and stir while bringing to a boil. Season with salt and pepper and set aside to cool.

3. Beat eggs in a separate bowl and whisk in the grated cheese(s) and mixed herbs. Pour into the cooled milk mixture. Then pour mixture into the buttered baking dish. Bake for 35–45 minutes or until the soufflé has puffed and is golden brown. Serve immediately.

MRS. EVERDEEN'S BREAKFAST OF MUSH

When indulging in her first breakfast in the Capitol, Katniss recalls her mom's "breakfast of mush," which here is made from hearty cornmeal, or its slightly thicker cousin, polenta. You can see that, while Mrs. Evergreen's oatmeal might not be as decadent as the Capitol dishes, love outshines all other ingredients. As this recipe suggests, home is where the heart is.
(*The Hunger Games*, Chapter 7)

Yields 6–8 servings

1 cup small or medium grain polenta

3 cups cold water

2 cups whole milk

1 teaspoon sea salt

½ cup brown sugar

2 teaspoons vanilla extract

1 teaspoon cinnamon

Heavy cream to taste

Cinnamon to taste

1 cup fresh blueberries

Tips from Your Sponsor

Polenta really is just another form of "mush"! Eaten in Roman times by peasants, it was known as *puls* or *pulmentum* in Latin, which roughly translates to "gruel" or "porridge" today. It only recently has become something of a staple in high-end fancy restaurants, and even those restaurants must work hard to transform this technically bland cornmeal into a delicious dish!

1. Mix together in a small bowl polenta and 1 cup cold water.

2. In a medium-sized saucepan, combine 2 cups cold water and 2 cups whole milk. Bring to a low boil over medium heat. Stir to combine.

3. Once the milk and water mixture begins to boil add sea salt and stir. Still stirring, slowly add the polenta and water mixture; be sure to whisk out any possible lumps.

4. Lower the heat and simmer the polenta, stirring frequently, until the mixture has thickened. Depending on the coarseness of the polenta, this may take anywhere between fifteen and thirty minutes.

5. Once the polenta has thickened, stir in brown sugar, vanilla extract, and 1 teaspoon cinnamon.

6. Ladle polenta into bowls. Add heavy cream and cinnamon to taste. Top with fresh blueberries and serve.

SMOKED GOUDA GRITS

If chefs in the Capitol got their hands on Mrs. Everdeen's Breakfast of Mush, chances are they'd take that simple recipe and turn it into something luxurious. Feel free to eat like a resident of the Capitol with this fancy recipe for grits.
(*The Hunger Games,* Chapter 7)

Yields 6 servings

1 cup quick-cooking grits

½ cup (1 stick) butter

8 ounces smoked Gouda, shredded

2 cloves garlic, minced

2 eggs

¾ cup whole milk

Tips from Your Sponsor

Grits are ground hominy. For this recipe, grits ground fine or medium-fine work best. Regular grits may be used in this recipe, too, as opposed to the quick-cooking variety. The smoked Gouda adds a new twist to classic Southern grits, but if you're not a Gouda fan try using other cheeses for a different flavor, such as creamy Camembert, blue cheese, or Gruyère.

1. Preheat oven to 350°F. Lightly grease a 2-quart baking dish and set aside.

2. In a large saucepan, cook grits according to manufacturer's directions. Remove from heat. Add butter and stir until melted. Stir in the cheese and garlic.

3. In a 2-cup measuring cup, beat the 2 eggs and add milk to measure 1 cup. Add to the cooled grits and stir to blend. Pour into greased casserole dish and bake for 40–45 minutes, until a knife inserted in the middle comes out clean. Serve hot.

APOCALYPTIC EGGS BENEDICT

An extremely rich dish, eggs Benedict is likely to be enjoyed by many inhabitants of the Capitol. So it stands to reason that when Katniss orders eggs for herself before training for the Quarter Quell, her simple request for "eggs" would be met by this lavish dish. The speed with which the eggs appear for Katniss can't help but make you think of the work that goes into finding food in the Seam—and the wastefulness of the Capitol. It's not a coincidence that wastefulness is what you think about right before Katniss heads out to the Quell. (*Catching Fire*, Chapter 16)

Yields 4 servings

4 slices bacon

2 teaspoons white vinegar

4 eggs

1 cup (2 sticks) butter

4 egg yolks

1 tablespoon heavy cream

1 teaspoon cayenne pepper

¼ teaspoon salt

1 tablespoon fresh lemon juice

4 English muffins, split, toasted, and buttered

Chopped chives, for garnish

Tips from Your Sponsor

There's no gray area when it comes to Eggs Benedict—you either love it or loathe it. If this recipe doesn't make you fall in love with Eggs Benedict, try it with smoked salmon or over corned beef instead of bacon. Or substitute cooked spinach and you have Eggs Florentine!

1. In a skillet over medium-high heat, fry bacon until browned. Set aside.

2. Fill a large saucepan with about three inches of water; bring water to simmer. Pour in the vinegar. Carefully break the eggs into the water, and cook for around 3 minutes, until whites are set but yolks are soft. Remove eggs with a slotted spoon and keep warm.

3. Melt butter. Do not brown but let butter remain warm.

4. Using a blender, blend the egg yolks, heavy cream, cayenne pepper, and salt until smooth. Add half the butter in a constant steady stream. Add lemon juice using the same method, followed by the rest of the butter.

5. Place English muffins on plates. Top with bacon, then egg, then drizzle with cream sauce. Garnish with chives.

TRASH TATERS

In *Catching Fire,* Katniss must battle more dread and betrayal than she does in *The Hunger Games.* Before meeting the other experienced tributes during training, Katniss orders a smorgasbord of breakfast choices, including these Trash Taters, which are made with unrefined ingredients to remind Katniss of her own humble beginnings while emotionally and physically warming her up for the trials ahead. (*Catching Fire,* Chapter 16)

Yields 4 servings

1 onion, chopped

1 ½ pounds lean ground beef

1 (10.75-ounce) can condensed cream of mushroom soup

1 (14.5-ounce) can drained French-style green beans

1 (32-ounce) package Tater Tots, thawed

3 teaspoons salt

3 teaspoons Italian seasoning

2 teaspoons garlic powder

3 teaspoons ground black pepper

Hot sauce to taste

2 cups shredded Cheddar cheese

1 (6-ounce) package French-fried onion rings

Tips from Your Sponsor

This is an everything and the kitchen sink type of recipe. If you have any vegetables lying around, such as red bell peppers, throw them in with the green beans for a delicious potato breakfast entrée!

1. Sauté onions until soft; add beef and cook until browned. Skim off any excess oil. Set aside.

2. Preheat oven to 350°F.

3. Spread mushroom soup and green beans at the bottom of a 9" x 13" baking dish.

4. Slowly add meat mixture to dish, then top with Tater Tots. Season with salt, Italian seasoning, garlic powder, black pepper, and hot sauce to taste. Top with 1 cup of Cheddar cheese. Add fried onion rings. Top with remaining Cheddar.

5. Bake at 350°F for 30–45 minutes, or until casserole is cooked through and brown at top.

In Spartan District 13, where there is no pleasure found in food and the motto is "waste not, want not," porridge, or hot grains, is an understandable and efficient breakfast.
(*Mockingjay*, Chapter 3)

Yields 4 servings

1 cup rolled oats

2½ cups water

1 teaspoon salt

1 tablespoon raisins

2 bananas, sliced

2 teaspoons cinnamon

1 tablespoon light brown sugar

1 tablespoon white sugar

½ cup cold milk (optional)

2 teaspoons honey (optional)

Tips from Your Sponsor

Hearty and filling, porridge was traditionally served with meats and a variety of roots. In District 13, however, such accoutrements would be seen as frivolous.

1. In a saucepan, combine the oats, water, salt, raisins, bananas, and cinnamon.

2. Bring to a boil, then reduce heat and simmer until the liquid has been absorbed, stirring frequently. Add sugars.

3. Pour concoction into bowls, then top each with milk and honey.

CHEESY MEATY HASH BROWN CASSEROLE

The bizarre yet nonetheless helpful Tigris makes this casserole for Katniss's team before their final showdown with the Capitol. This filling breakfast treat, when viewed in comparison to other breakfasts that Katniss has enjoyed in the Capitol, is symbolic of the current, depressed state of affairs in the city. (*Mockingjay*, Chapter 24)

Yields 12 servings

1 (32-ounce) package frozen hash brown potatoes

8 ounces cooked, diced ham

8 ounces cooked bacon, crumbled

2 (10.75-ounce) cans cream of potato soup

¼ cup onions, chopped

¼ cup green bell pepper, chopped

¼ cup red bell pepper, chopped

1 (16-ounce) container sour cream

½ teaspoon nutmeg

2 cups shredded medium Cheddar cheese

1 cup shredded sharp Cheddar cheese

Tips from Your Sponsor

For a variation on this treat, try grated Parmesan baked on top of the casserole instead of sharp Cheddar cheese. Or, sauté 2 cups of flaked corn cereal in 1 cup butter and place *that* on top of your casserole for a crunchier bite!

1. Preheat oven to 350°F. Lightly grease a 9" x 13" baking dish.

2. In a large bowl, mix together the hash browns, ham, bacon, cream of potato soup, onions, bell peppers, sour cream, nutmeg, and medium Cheddar cheese. Spread evenly into prepared dish. Sprinkle with sharp Cheddar cheese.

3. Bake 1 hour in the preheated oven, or until bubbly and light brown. Serve immediately.

DON'T PUT ALL YOUR EGGS IN ONE BASKET: EGG AND SAUSAGE PIE

Not all pies need be sweet. This savory pie closely resembles a breakfast quiche, though it can be enjoyed for dinner, too. Such a simple hearty dish is likely known and cooked by Greasy Sae while caring for Katniss after the destruction of the Capitol. The food here would be familiar from Katniss's youth and would comfort her. (*Mockingjay*, Chapter 27)

Yields 8 servings

½ pound Italian sausage

1 tablespoon extra-virgin olive oil

3 eggs

1 (10-ounce) pack frozen chopped spinach, thawed and thoroughly squeezed dry

2 cups fresh mozzarella cheese, shredded

½ cup pecorino Romano cheese, shredded

1 cup ricotta cheese

1 teaspoon kosher salt

2 cloves garlic, minced

1 yellow onion, diced

1 teaspoon oregano

¼ teaspoon freshly ground black pepper

¼ teaspoon cayenne pepper

1 (10") pastry for a double-crust pie

1 tablespoon water

Tips from Your Sponsor

This egg pie leaves you room to experiment. If you're tired of Pecorino Romano try using Asiago or Manchego cheese. Mushrooms are also an excellent addition. Try serving with fresh salsa—the tomatoes greatly complement the eggs and spinach.

1. In a skillet, cook sausage with olive oil over medium heat until sausage is no longer pink; drain and set aside.

2. Separate one egg and set the yolk aside. In a mixing bowl, beat egg white with remaining 2 eggs. Add spinach, mozzarella cheese, pecorino Romano cheese, ricotta, salt, garlic, diced onion, and cooked sausage. Mix well. Add oregano, black pepper, and cayenne pepper.

3. Line a 10" pie plate with the bottom pastry. Add filling. Roll out remaining pastry to fit top of pie and place over filling. Trim, seal, and flute edges. Cut slits in pastry. Beat water and remaining egg yolk; brush over top.

4. Bake at 350°F for 60–75 minutes or until crust is golden brown and the juices are bubbling through the slits. Let stand for 15 minutes before cutting.

CHAPTER 2

BREAKING BREAD

Of all the foods described in The Hunger Games trilogy, bread is by far the most mentioned—and the most important. Bread is *everywhere* in the Hunger Games. It's a form of national pride and national identity (each District has its own distinct bread), and grain is one of the few meager offerings given to those poor souls who put themselves up for Tesserae, which showcases the class struggle seen throughout the books. While some breads are finer than others, every citizen of Panem, from the elites in the Capitol to the mineworkers in District 11, would vouch for its necessity.

FRENCH BREAD FROM THE MELLARK FAMILY BAKERY

Before we are even introduced to Peeta, we're introduced to his family's bakery: Gale arrives at his and Katniss's pre–Reaping Day hunt, a loaf of bread with an arrow shot through it in hand. Katniss can't help but smile. After all, "it's real bakery bread . . . fine bread like this is for special occasions." The fact that bread is mentioned so early in the book foreshadows the importance it will take on as the story unfolds.
(*The Hunger Games*, Chapter 1)

Yields 2 large loaves

5½ cups all-purpose flour

1 (.25-ounce) package or 5 teaspoons active dry yeast

2 tablespoons butter, softened

3 teaspoons salt

2 cups warm water (110°F)

1 tablespoon cornmeal

1 egg

1 tablespoon water

2 tablespoons butter

1 tablespoon honey

1. In a large bowl, combine 2 cups flour, yeast, 2 tablespoons softened butter, and salt. Stir in 2 cups warm water, and, preferably using a stand mixer with a dough hook attachment, beat until well blended. Using a wooden spoon, stir in as much of the remaining flour as you can.

2. On a lightly floured surface, knead in enough flour to make a stiff dough that is also smooth and elastic. Knead for 8–10 minutes total. Shape into a ball. Place dough in a greased bowl, and turn over to thoroughly coat ball. Cover, and let rise in a warm place until doubled, about 1 hour.

3. Punch dough down, and divide in half. Place back on the lightly floured surface. Cover, and let rise for 15 minutes.

4. Roll each half into a large rectangle. Roll up, starting from the long side. Moisten edge with water and seal. Taper the ends.

5. Preheat oven to 375°F.

6. Grease a large baking sheet. Sprinkle with cornmeal. Place loaves, seam side down, on the baking sheet.

7. In a small bowl, lightly beat the egg with the water. Brush about half of mixture over the loaves. With a sharp knife, make 4 shallow diagonal cuts across the top of each loaf. Cover with a damp cloth. Let rise until nearly doubled, about 45 minutes.

8. Bake at 375°F for 20 minutes. Remove from oven, and brush each loaf again with egg mixture. Bake for an additional 20 minutes, or until bread appears done.

9. Five minutes before bread should be done, melt 2 tablespoons butter and add honey.

10. When bread is lightly browned, remove from baking sheet. Pour honey-butter mixture over bread, and lightly place a sheet of aluminum foil over each loaf. Place a damp towel over loaves. Let sit for fifteen minutes. Finish cooling on a wire rack.

Tips from Your Sponsor

While not necessary with this recipe, to make truly *French* French bread, throw a couple handfuls of ice cubes in a pan at the bottom of your oven a few seconds before putting in the bread. Many chefs swear that the evaporation helps makes for an extra-crunchy crust and moist middle.

THE BOY WITH THE BREAD: HEARTY RAISIN NUT BREAD

When they first meet, Peeta gives Katniss a hearty raisin and nut bread that literally saves Katniss's life. This story not only showcases the emotional connection between the novels' heroes and food, but also foreshadows the importance that bread holds throughout the trilogy.
(*The Hunger Games,* Chapter 2)

Yields 2 large loaves

1 (.25-ounce) package or 5 teaspoons active dry yeast

½ cup warm water (110°F)

1½ cups warm milk (110°F)

½ cup (1 stick) butter, melted

1/3 cup honey

2 teaspoons salt

2 teaspoons ground cinnamon

2 teaspoons white sugar

2 eggs

3 cups whole wheat flour

3½ cups all-purpose flour

2 cups raisins

1 cup chopped walnuts

1 egg white

2 tablespoons cold water

Tips from Your Sponsor

To give this hearty bread a sweeter taste, add 2 more teaspoons ground cinnamon and 2 tablespoons sugar to the mixture.

1. In a mixing bowl, dissolve yeast in the warm water until foamy, about 5 minutes. Add the milk, butter, honey, salt, cinnamon, sugar, eggs, and whole wheat flour. Beat until smooth. Stir in enough all-purpose flour to form a soft dough.

2. Place raisins in a bowl of tepid tap water. Let soak until needed.

3. Turn dough out onto a floured surface; knead until smooth and elastic, about 10 minutes. Place in a greased bowl, turning once to coat. Cover with a damp towel and let rise in a warm place until doubled, about 1 hour.

4. Grease two 8.5" × 4.5" loaf pans.

5. Punch dough down. Turn out onto the lightly floured surface; sprinkle with raisins and walnuts and knead them in. Divide dough in half.

6. Roll dough into loaves, keeping raisins folded inside.

7. Place loaves into greased loaf pans. Cover and let rise until doubled, about one hour.

8. Preheat oven to 375°F.

9. Beat egg white and cold water; brush over loaves.

10. Bake at 375°F for 40 minutes or until golden brown. If top browns too quickly, cover loosely with foil for the last 15 minutes.

11. Remove from pans to wire racks to cool.

KATNISS-APPROVED PUFFY BUTTERMILK BISCUITS

Using a mouthpiece that magically appears when Katniss opens the menu in her Capitol living quarters, Katniss orders this dish along with a side of goose liver. But when the puffy bread can't quench Katniss's hunger, we see that it's a metaphor for the Capitol itself: full of hot air.
(*The Hunger Games,* Chapter 6)

Yields 1 dozen biscuits

3 cups all-purpose flour

3 tablespoons white sugar

4 teaspoons baking powder

1 teaspoon salt

1 teaspoon baking soda

1 cup (2 sticks) chilled unsalted butter, cut into pieces

1¼ cups buttermilk

Tips from Your Sponsor

These biscuits taste great on their own, with Goose Liver Pâté or Liver Pâté, or with a dollop of Mixed Messages Mixed Berry Jam (see Chapter 4)! Looking for something other than corn bread to serve with chili? Try these!

1. Preheat oven to 425°F.

2. Blend flour, sugar, baking powder, salt, and baking soda in a large bowl.

3. Using fingertips, rub chilled butter into dry ingredients until mixture resembles coarse meal. Add buttermilk and stir until evenly moistened.

4. Using ¼ cup dough for each biscuit, drop biscuits onto a well-greased baking sheet, spacing about 2 inches apart. Using a spoon, flatten top of each biscuit. Bake until biscuits are golden brown on top, about 15 minutes. Cool slightly. Serve warm.

DISTRICT 12 DROP BISCUITS

While admiring the various districts' bread displayed prominently at her training, Katniss comments on her own district's bread, calling them "ugly drop biscuits." However, she's not really talking about bread here. Instead, she's doubting her own worth and comparing herself to the large, muscular tributes that she'll soon be facing in the arena.
(*The Hunger Games*, Chapter 7)

Yields 1 dozen biscuits

1 cup all-purpose flour

1 cup whole wheat flour

1 tablespoon baking powder

2 tablespoons white sugar

1 teaspoon salt

½ cup (1 stick) cold unsalted butter, thinly sliced

1 cup milk

1. Preheat oven to 450°F. Lightly grease a baking sheet.

2. In a large bowl, thoroughly combine flours, baking powder, sugar, and salt. Using your fingertips, pinch in butter until mixture forms coarse crumbs. Add milk, mixing until just barely moistened.

3. Drop batter on baking sheet by the tablespoon.

4. Bake in preheated oven until edges of biscuits are golden, 8–10 minutes. Serve warm.

Tips from Your Sponsor

For a sweeter treat, try spreading Mixed Messages Mixed Berry Jam (Chapter 4), From Casual to Formal: Fruit Nut Spread at the Capitol Banquet (Chapter 4), or even butter on top of your biscuit before eating! It is also possible to add an extra tablespoon of sugar to this recipe if your sweet tooth is not satisfied by the levels of sugar already recommended. Keep in mind, though, that in England, a *biscuit* commonly refers to a small and unsweetened flour-based product, like a cracker. It's the "American" who gave *biscuits* their sweetness.

DISTRICT 11'S CRESCENT MOON ROLL WITH SESAME SEEDS

District 11 specializes in agriculture and, even though the harsh Peacekeepers don't allow their citizens much time to garden on their own, their bread is representative of their District's culture. The sesame seeds that coat this crescent moon-shaped bread showcase the reaping and sowing of District 11's main crop.
(*The Hunger Games*, Chapter 7 and 18)

Yields 8–16 rolls

2 (.25-ounce) packages active dry yeast

¾ cup warm water (110°F)

½ cup plus 2 tablespoons white sugar

1 teaspoon salt

2 eggs

½ cup (1 stick) butter, thinly sliced and
  room temperature

2 cups all-purpose flour

2 cups whole wheat flour

¼ cup butter, melted

1 large egg

1 tablespoon milk

2 tablespoons sesame seeds

Tips from Your Sponsor

Ever wonder why so many bread recipes call for kneading? Kneading develops long elastic strands of gluten, the wheat protein, which trap the gases produced by the yeast. Without these elastic strands, bread would not have the texture and chewiness we so enjoy.

1. In a large bowl, dissolve yeast in warm water.

2. Mix in sugar, salt, eggs, butter, 1 cup all-purpose flour, and 1 cup whole wheat flour. Beat until smooth, about 5 minutes. Add remaining all-purpose and whole wheat flours, and mix until smooth again.

3. Scrape dough from sides of bowl. Using your hands, knead dough for ten minutes on a lightly floured surface, then place in a well-greased bowl. Cover bowl and let bread rise in a warm place until it doubles in size, about 1½–2 hours.

4. Grease a large baking sheet.

5. Punch down dough. Divide in half. Roll each half into a 12" circle. Spread melted butter over each circle.

6. Cut circles in half to yield 8–16 triangle-shaped wedges. Roll up wedges starting at the wide end. Curve edges to make a crescent shape. Place rolls with small pointed side down, 2 inches apart on greased baking sheet. Cover and let rise until doubled, at least 90 minutes (preferably 2 hours).

7. Preheat oven to 375°F.

8. Combine 1 large egg with 1 tablespoon milk. Brush rolls with egg glaze and sprinkle with sesame seeds. Bake rolls at 375°F for 10–12 minutes or until golden brown.

SUPER SWEET POTATO ROLLS

When Katniss ambivalently kisses Peeta in the arena, Haymitch (and the sponsors) reward Katniss with a basket of delicacies including these delicious sweet rolls. The food Haymitch sends along acts as a secret message to show Katniss what he'd like to see from her; in this case, more sweetness! (*The Hunger Games*, Chapter 22)

Yields 1½ dozen rolls

1 (.25 ounce) package active dry yeast

2 tablespoons white sugar

½ cup warm water (110°F)

4 tablespoons brown sugar

1 teaspoon ground nutmeg

1 teaspoon ground cinnamon

3 medium sweet potatoes, baked, peeled, and mashed with a fork

3 tablespoons butter, softened

1 teaspoon salt

2 eggs, slightly beaten

3¼ cups all-purpose flour

Tips from Your Sponsor

If you're short on time, instead of baking sweet potatoes and then mashing them by hand, just buy a 15-ounce can of sweet potato purée and use half of it in this recipe. Use the rest of the can for a yummy sweet potato pie!

1. Preheat oven to 375°F. Grease a large baking sheet.

2. In a mixing bowl, dissolve yeast and 1 tablespoon white sugar in the warm water. Let stand 10 minutes, until foamy.

3. Add remaining white sugar, brown sugar, sweet potato, butter, salt, and eggs. Stir to mix well.

4. In a bowl, whisk nutmeg and cinnamon in with 3 cups flour. Add flour mixture to sweet potato mixture.

5. Turn out on a lightly floured surface. Knead 3 minutes, adding just enough of remaining flour to prevent sticking. Do not knead too heavily. When smooth, shape into a ball. Place in a well-oiled bowl, and turn to coat the surface. Cover, and let rise for at least 1 hour, preferably 1½ hours.

6. Punch down dough, and allow to rest for 3 minutes. Divide into 18 small balls, and place on the greased cookie sheet. Cover lightly with plastic wrap and allow dough to rise until doubled, about 1 hour.

7. Bake at 375°F for 15–20 minutes. Serve warm, with butter.

MOCKINGJAY FLATBREAD CRACKERS

When Katniss finds Twill hiding in her cabin on the lake, Katniss is all ready to shoot her—until she sees that Twill is holding a flatbread cracker with a mockingjay carved into it. Here the bread represents a token of hope and, more importantly, goodwill.
(*Catching Fire*, Chapter 9 and 10)

Yields about 1 dozen crackers

1½ cups all-purpose flour

1½ cups whole wheat flour

¼ cup vegetable oil

1½ teaspoons baking soda

1 teaspoon kosher salt

¾–1 cup buttermilk, room temperature

1 teaspoon almond extract

Tips from Your Sponsor

To spice up this basic recipe, try mixing a pinch of cloves and cinnamon, or garlic powder and onion powder, or even a ½ cup of cheese into the flour! This flatbread goes well with hummus or any Middle Eastern–esque topping.

1. Preheat oven to 350°F. Lightly grease a large cookie sheet.

2. In a large bowl combine all-purpose flour, whole wheat flour, oil, baking soda, and salt.

3. In a small bowl, whisk together buttermilk and almond extract. Add enough buttermilk mixture to the flour mixture to make a stiff yet not too moist dough.

4. Knead dough for one minute on a well-floured surface.

5. Cover dough. Roll 1/3-cup handfuls of dough into small balls between your hands and pat each into a small circle. Using a rolling pin, flatten the 1/3-cup handfuls of dough into 10" circles. Place onto greased cookie sheet. Bake in preheated oven for 10–12 minutes; the longer they bake, the crisper the crackers.

PEETA'S CINNAMON BAKERY BREAD

After a stressful interview with the Peacekeepers, Katniss falls asleep while leaning against Peeta, who smells like the cinnamon and dill of his bakery breads. To Katniss, these smells represent safety, security, and home—and the description of these smells juxtaposes Katniss and Peeta's terrifying reality with the safe life they crave.
(*Catching Fire*, Chapter 11)

Yields 1 large bundt loaf

2 cups all-purpose flour

1 cup white sugar

2 teaspoons baking powder

½ teaspoon baking soda

2 teaspoons ground cinnamon

1 teaspoon kosher salt

1 cup buttermilk

¼ cup vegetable oil

2 eggs

3 teaspoons vanilla extract

2 tablespoons white sugar

2 tablespoons brown sugar

2 teaspoons ground cinnamon

2 tablespoons butter

Tips from Your Sponsor

Don't have buttermilk in your kitchen? Here's a handy substitution for regular buttermilk: Pour 1 tablespoon lemon juice or white vinegar into a measuring cup, and then add regular milk up to the 1-cup mark. Let stand for five minutes, then use as much as your recipe calls for! (In this case, you would use the whole cup.)

1. Preheat oven to 350°F. Grease one regular-sized bundt pan.

2. Mix flour, 1 cup white sugar, baking powder, baking soda, cinnamon, and salt in a large bowl. In a separate bowl, mix buttermilk, vegetable oil, eggs, and vanilla. Combine wet and dry ingredients, mixing thoroughly by hand for at least 3 minutes.

3. In a small bowl, combine 2 tablespoons white sugar, 2 tablespoons brown sugar, cinnamon, and butter. Mix until crumbly.

4. Pour half of the wet flour mixture into prepared bundt pan. Sprinkle half of the brown sugar/butter mixture evenly on top of flour mixture; pour rest of flour mixture over topping. Smooth batter and remaining topping over it. Using a knife, swirl topping for a marbled effect.

5. Bake for 45 minutes to an hour. Bread is finished when a toothpick inserted in the center comes out clean. Let cool for 10 minutes, then remove from pan to rack to finish cooling.

HEAVENLY ONION & DILL BREAD

Peeta, a living symbol of pure goodness for Katniss, often smells like the breads he bakes. This cottage bread (a form of hearty white bread) is full of particularly pungent ingredients such as onion and dill. Thus, it makes sense that when Peeta goes to comfort a hurt Katniss, the scent of the bread follows him—a comforting and calming smell that makes Katniss feel safe.
(*Catching Fire*, Chapter 11)

Yields 2 loaves

2 envelopes active dry yeast

1 cup warm water (about 105°F)

2 cups bread flour

3 tablespoons sugar

1 tablespoon kosher salt

¼ teaspoon baking soda

12 ounces cottage cheese, small curd

1½ tablespoons fresh dill, minced

1 egg

½ cup Parmesan cheese, grated

1 tablespoon fresh onion, finely minced

½ cup (1 stick) butter, melted

1 teaspoon coarse salt

Tips from Your Sponsor

Not sure if your dough has doubled? Try lightly dipping a finger in flour and press in the middle of the dough. If the hole stays indented, it's done rising. If it springs back, it still has more rising to accomplish!

1. In a large bowl, combine yeast and warm water. Let stand until yeast is dissolved.

2. Into a large bowl, sift bread flour, sugar, salt, and baking soda. Thoroughly mix. Add yeast mixture, cottage cheese, dill, and egg. Mix until dough comes together, adding more flour or water if necessary. Knead by hand for 10 minutes or until dough becomes smooth and elastic.

3. Place dough onto a lightly floured surface. Fold in Parmesan cheese and onion; knead for five minutes.

4. Place dough in a well-oiled bowl. Cover gently with plastic wrap. Let rise until doubled, at least 1–2 hours.

5. Thoroughly grease two 12" bread pans. Return dough to lightly floured surface. Lightly press down to shape bread, then divide dough in half. Place dough in bread pans. Cover with oiled plastic wrap. Let rise in a warm place until doubled again in volume, at least 1 hour.

6. Preheat oven to 350°F.

7. Pour ¼ cup melted butter over each loaf, and sprinkle each with ½ teaspoon coarse salt. Place in preheated oven and bake for 45–50 minutes, or until brown. Let cool before serving.

DISTRICT 4'S SEAWEED BREAD

As with most of the District's breads, the seaweed bread unique to District 4 is representative of that District's specialty. The slightly green bread is indicative of the living those in District 4 earn from the sea. (*Catching Fire*, Chapter 22)

Yields 1 loaf

1 cup white bread flour

1 cup whole wheat four

1 (.25-ounce) package or 5 teaspoons active dry yeast

1½ cups warm water

5 teaspoons coarse kosher or sea salt

2 tablespoons granulated sugar

5 teaspoons or .45 ounces dehydrated wakame seaweed weighed/measured before soaking (soak in warm water for 20 minutes, drain, and cut into small pieces)

Tips from Your Sponsor

Bread is one of the trickiest foods any baker can make, but like Katniss's skill with the bow and arrow, it's really just a matter of getting a feel for it. Luckily, practice makes perfect! Some helpful tips: Fully baked bread is firm to the touch and browned all over. If it's spongy, then it's underdone . . . so just throw it back in the oven! Another test is to slide the loaf from the pan and tap the bottom of the bread lightly with your fingers. If you hear a hollow sound, that means it's done and ready to eat.

1. Stir together both flours in a large bowl. Stir in the yeast. Add water and mix the ingredients by hand until they form a wet, sticky dough.

2. Cover the mixing bowl and dough with plastic wrap or a damp towel. Let the dough rest for 30 minutes (this technique is called autolyze). Do not be surprised if it expands; it's supposed to!

3. Turn the dough out onto a floured work surface and flatten gently with your hands. Sprinkle the salt and sugar over the dough and knead the dough for 5–7 minutes, until smooth and elastic. Add seaweed and continue kneading until it is evenly distributed throughout the dough.

4. Coat another large bowl with oil. Shape the dough into a ball and place it in the bowl. Cover with either a damp towel or plastic wrap and let rise for 45 minutes. It should almost double in size.

5. After 45 minutes, take out the ball and pat it gently (take care not to flatten it, as this will compress the air bubbles, making for a heavier bread) and turn it over. Return to bowl and let rise, covered, another 45 minutes. Repeat the process for another 45-minute rise. Turning the dough will give your bread a nice airy structure.

6. Lightly flour a baking sheet. Turn the dough out onto the sheet and gently mold it into an oval shape. (Go ahead and use a rolling pin if need be, though using your hands is more fun.) Lightly cover the bread with plastic wrap. Be sure to leave enough space between plastic wrap and bread for the dough to expand in size.

7. Let the covered dough rise for 1 hour until it is almost doubled in size.

8. Preheat the oven to 475°F.

9. Remove plastic wrap. Transfer baking sheet and bread to middle rack in oven. Bake the loaf 45 minutes until evenly browned. Remove from the oven. Let cool for at least half an hour before slicing.

DISTRICT 3 DINNER ROLLS

The District 3 Dinner Rolls showcase the District's technological capabilities. This District is known for its aptitude with electronics, and the square-shaped dinner rolls serve to distance the District from the natural world that so many other Districts rely upon heavily. (*Catching Fire*, Chapter 24)

Yields about 16 rolls

1 envelope (.25-ounce) active dry yeast

½ cup white sugar

½ cup warm water (110°F)

½ cup whole milk

¾ cup (1 ½ sticks) butter, softened

1 egg

4 cups all-purpose flour

2 teaspoons sea salt

Tips from Your Sponsor

For a non-square-roll: When dough is placed on a lightly floured surface, divide dough ball in half. Roll each half into a 12" circle, and spread 2 tablespoons softened butter over each round. Cut each circle into 8 to 10 small triangles. Roll wedges starting at the wider end; roll gently but tightly. Place wedges point side down on well-greased cookie sheet. Cover and let rise for 1 hour.

1. Generously oil a baking sheet.

2. In a small bowl, dissolve active dry yeast and 1 tablespoon of the sugar in the warm water. Let sit for 10 minutes, until foamy.

3. Warm the milk in a saucepan over medium heat until it bubbles around the edges. Remove from heat; stir in remaining sugar and ½ cup of the butter until melted. Let cool to lukewarm.

4. In a large bowl, combine yeast mixture, milk mixture, salt, and egg. Stir in flour ½ cup at a time.

5. Place dough on a lightly floured surface. Knead dough for 8 minutes. Gently flatten.

6. Spread remaining ¼ cup softened butter over flattened dough and fold dough in half. Break off 2"–3" pieces of dough, roll each lightly into a ball, and place the dough balls in a rectangular pattern on oiled baking sheet or square baking ban, edges touching. Repeat to make one to two dozen dough balls, depending on size of pieces. Cover with clean kitchen towel and place baking sheet in a warm place. Let rise 1 hour until doubled in size.

7. Preheat oven to 400°F.

8. Bake dough in preheated oven for 10–15 minutes, until golden.

DISTRICT 13'S NO-NONSENSE WHEAT DINNER ROLLS

District 13 survives on a "waste not, want not" philosophy, which makes this utilitarian wheat roll perfect for this District.
(*Mockingjay*, Chapter 4)

Yields 2 dozen rolls

2 (.25-ounce) packages active dry yeast

1¾ cups warm water (110°F)

1 cup white sugar

2 teaspoons salt

1cup (2 sticks) butter, melted and cooled

1 egg, beaten

2½ cups whole wheat flour

2 cups all-purpose flour

Tips from Your Sponsor

Is your dough too sticky to handle? Try rubbing your hands in oil or even water before managing the dough. This makes handling it easier, as does having a wet bench scraper.

1. In a large bowl, dissolve yeast in warm water. Let stand until creamy, about 10 minutes.

2. Mix sugar, salt, ½ cup of the butter, egg, and whole wheat flour into yeast mixture. Stir in all-purpose flour, ¼ cup at a time, until dough pulls away from the sides of the bowl. Turn dough out onto a well-floured surface, and knead until smooth and elastic, about 8 minutes.

3. Lightly oil a large bowl, place dough in bowl, and turn to coat. Cover with a damp cloth and let rise in a warm place until doubled in volume, at least 1 hour.

4. Punch down dough, cover, and let rise in warm place until doubled again, about another hour.

5. Grease 24 muffin cups. Punch down dough, but do not knead, and divide into two equal portions. Roll each into a 6" x 14" rectangle, and cut rectangle into twelve 7" x 1" strips. Roll strips up into spirals, and place one spiral into each muffin cup. Brush tops with ½ cup melted butter. Let rise uncovered in a warm place for about 1 hour, or until doubled in size.

6. Preheat oven to 400°F. Bake for 10–15 minutes, or until golden brown. Remove from oven, and brush again with ¼ cup melted butter.

KATNISS'S CRAVED CHEESE BUNS

Katniss loves Peeta's family's cheese buns, and throughout The Hunger Games trilogy the buns become a symbol of home and of Katniss and Peeta's lives before they became tributes. This symbolism is so pervasive that Katniss's preference for cheese buns becomes part of Peeta and Katniss's "Real or Not Real" game to help Peeta find himself after the Capitol violated and changed his memories. (*Mockingjay*, Chapter 19)

Yields 1 dozen buns

2 cups Bisquick

¼ teaspoon garlic powder

¼ cup sugar

2/3 cup milk

¾ cup sharp Cheddar cheese, shredded

½ cup (1 stick) butter

½ teaspoon garlic powder

½ teaspoon Old Bay Seasoning

½ teaspoon kosher salt

Tips from Your Sponsor

Cheese buns are a popular snack and breakfast food in Brazil and areas of northern Argentina, though in those places the buns are commonly made with corn flour and Minas cheese, yielding a less sweet yet similarly moist treat!

1. Preheat oven to 450°F. Grease a cookie sheet.

2. Mix Bisquick, 1/3 teaspoon garlic powder, sugar, milk, and cheese until well blended.

3. Drop by spoonfuls onto greased cookie sheet.

4. Bake 8–10 minutes.

5. In a microwave-safe bowl, combine butter, ½ teaspoon garlic powder, Old Bay seasoning, and kosher salt. Heat in microwave for 30 seconds, until butter is melted.

6. Generously brush tops of biscuits with butter mixture.

CHAPTER 3

KEEP THE CAMP FIRES LOW AND FORAGE-SOUPS, STEWS, AND SALADS

While soups, stews, and salads might sound like a hodgepodge of side dishes, in The Hunger Games trilogy, more often than not, they're eaten as a main dish. The side dishes that you'll find here are as different as the Districts from which they come, with (Wild Dog Optional) Beef Stew from the Seam representing the hard life of those in the Seam and the elegant Capitol Cream of Pumpkin Soup with Slivered Nuts and Cinnamon Croutons showcasing the luxurious lifestyle enjoyed by those in the Capitol. But no matter where the dish comes from, it embodies kindness on the behalf of the giver. The types of side dishes given casually and gratefully received throughout The Hunger Games trilogy are mostly comfort foods that are designed to uplift the soul and give the characters the heart they need to face the tragedies they're forced to endure. The soups, stews, and even salads found in this chapter can warm the soul on days when everything feels cold no matter the temperature.

[WILD DOG OPTIONAL] BEEF STEW FROM THE SEAM

Greasy Sae, perhaps best known for her filling (albeit questionable) stews, is one of the few citizens of the Seam who will buy wild dog from Katniss and Gale. Recipes such as this illustrate the hardiness of those who live in the Seam. After all, you are what you eat and nothing is more wild or brave than wild dog. However, if you prefer your dogs at the ends of leashes and not at the end of a spoon, here's a delicious beef stew recipe—wild dog optional.
(*The Hunger Games,* Chapter 1)

Yields 6–8 servings

½ cup all-purpose flour

1 teaspoon kosher salt

1 teaspoon fresh ground pepper

2 pounds stew beef (or wild dog meat), cubed

¼ cup water

2 tablespoons cornstarch

2 tablespoons vegetable oil

1 cup water

1½ cups beef broth

2 tablespoons Worcestershire sauce

1 clove garlic, peeled

2 bay leaves

1 medium onion, sliced

1 teaspoon white sugar

1 teaspoon dark brown sugar

2 teaspoons paprika

1 teaspoon ground allspice

3 large carrots, sliced

3 ribs celery, chopped

5 russet potatoes, cubed

Tips from Your Sponsor

One of the great things about a good, hearty stew is that you can put practically any vegetable you want in it. Not a fan of carrots? Feel free to replace them with mushrooms, or asparagus, or both. Just be careful of pot overflow!

Not a fan of thick stew? For a thinner stew, skip the cornstarch mixture. Just add the vegetables to the pot after the 90 minutes of cooking and then continue cooking for the additional 45 minutes. Voilà!—a lighter, but nevertheless delicious, stew.

1. In a medium bowl, combine flour, salt, and fresh ground pepper. Pour flour mixture into a gallon-size Ziploc bag. Place meat cubes into Ziploc bag; shake cubes in bag to thoroughly coat.

2. In a small bowl, mix ¼ cup water and cornstarch. Set aside.

3. Oil and heat a large skillet. Place floured beef into skillet and sauté until browned.

4. Remove meat from skillet and place in large pot. Add 1 cup water, beef broth, Worcestershire sauce, garlic, bay leaves, onions, sugars, paprika, and allspice. Cover and cook over low heat for 90 minutes. Remove bay leaves and garlic cloves; discard. Ladle out about 1 cup of stew liquid and stir it into the cornstarch mixture. Stir the cornstarch–stew liquid combination back into the pot.

5. Add carrots, celery, and potatoes to pot. Cover and cook for another 30–45 minutes, then stir and mix until thick and bubbly, about fifteen minutes. Remove from heat and enjoy once cooled.

PRIM'S SWEET GOAT CHEESE SALAD

Historically, goats represent sacrifice and giving. When Prim sells most of her goat cheese at the Hob, she sacrifices so her family can eat. However, she could easily make this salad for her own family using natural ingredients found by her sister or Gale in the forbidden woods. (*The Hunger Games*, Chapter 3)

Yields 4 servings

3 cups fresh romaine lettuce

½ cup fresh blueberries

½ cup fresh raspberries

¼ cup dried cranberries

½ cup sunflower seeds

¼ cup pecans, chopped

½ cup goat cheese, crumbled

¼ cup white balsamic vinegar

¼ cup maple syrup

¼ cup olive oil

Sea salt to taste

Tips from Your Sponsor

You can cut the strong goat cheese taste by using ¼ cup goat cheese and ¼ cup feta cheese. If you're a nut fan, add an additional ¼ cup walnuts for a delicious mixed salad.

1. Toss the romaine lettuce, blueberries, raspberries, dried cranberries, sunflower seeds, pecans, and goat cheese in a large bowl.

2. Pour the vinegar, maple syrup, and olive oil over the salad, toss until evenly coated. Season with salt.

GINGER, CARROT, AND BUTTERNUT SQUASH SOUP

It's not surprising that this thick and creamy (and yet practically creamless) soup was served at Katniss and Peeta's first dinner away from home. Soup is usually looked at as a comfort food and comfort is the one thing Katniss and Peeta desperately desired on the trip to the Capitol. (*The Hunger Games*, Chapter 3)

Yields 6 servings

1 medium butternut squash

4 tablespoons olive oil

1 onion, diced

3 cloves garlic, crushed

4 cups chicken or vegetable stock

1 teaspoon orange zest

Juice of 1 orange

1½ pounds carrots, peeled and diced

2 (2") pieces fresh gingerroot, peeled and thinly sliced

3 teaspoons ground cinnamon

1 teaspoon nutmeg

2 teaspoons sugar

Salt and white pepper to taste

¼ cup heavy cream

Tips from Your Sponsor

For a complete meal, try the District 3 Dinner Rolls (Chapter 2) or Super Sweet Potato Rolls (Chapter 2) as a side to this clearly filling soup.

1. Preheat the oven to 350°F. Grease a baking sheet.

2. Cut butternut squash in half. Scoop seeds out of the squash, and place cut side down onto greased baking sheet. Discard seeds. Bake for 40 minutes, or until softened. Remove from oven. Once cooled, scoop squash flesh out of the skin using a large wooden spoon. Set flesh aside; discard skin.

3. In a large stockpot, heat the olive oil. Add onion and garlic; cook, stirring frequently, until onion appears translucent. Add stock, orange zest, orange juice, squash, carrots, and ginger. Bring to a boil, and cook for at least 30 minutes, or until carrots and ginger are tender.

4. Using an immersion blender for a creamier mixture or a potato masher for a chunkier one, blend or mash the soup. Return soup to pot, and heat through. Stir in cinnamon, nutmeg, and sugar. Season with salt and pepper.

5. Ladle into bowls; pour a thin swirl of cream over the top.

GREASY SAE'S SPICY VEGETARIAN CHILI

Sometimes that poverty in the Seam is so dire there's no meat (not even dog entrails) for Greasy Sae to use in her hearty soups. However, this chili, while lacking in meat, more than makes up for it in flavor.
(*The Hunger Games*, Chapter 3)

Yields 4–6 servings

3 tablespoons olive oil

1 large yellow onion, sliced

1 clove garlic, diced

1 teaspoon cumin (more to taste)

2 cups vegetable broth

6 plum tomatoes, diced

2 jalapeño peppers with seeds, sliced

1 yellow pepper, sliced

1 red pepper, sliced

5 chipotle peppers (canned), sliced

1 8-ounce pack fresh white mushrooms

1 teaspoon chili powder

1 12-ounce can tomato paste

1 10-ounce pack vegetable crumbles (found in freezer section)

1 15-ounce can kidney beans, drained

1 15-ounce can pinto beans, drained

1 15-ounce can black beans, drained

Kosher salt to taste

Ground black pepper to taste

1. In a large pan, heat olive oil over medium-high heat. Cook sliced onion, diced garlic, and cumin in olive oil until lightly browned. Add vegetable broth, plum tomatoes, all the peppers, white mushrooms, chili powder, and tomato paste. Mix thoroughly, then cover and let simmer for 45 minutes.

2. Add vegetable crumbles to mixture and let simmer for 20 minutes. Add all the beans and let the whole thing cook over very low heat for at least 60 minutes. Add salt and pepper and extra cumin to taste.

Tips from Your Sponsor

This recipe isn't for the faint-hearted (thus making it perfect for Katniss). The amounts of spices and peppers in this recipe pack quite a punch. For less spice, use only 2 chipotle peppers.

The fact that Katniss can hold down this gross-sounding dish while feeling ill after eating just one meal of rich foods from the Capitol shows how Katniss is used to hard living; she's not at home in the lap of luxury. The fact that the meal from the Capitol makes her ill also shows that she's having a hard time stomaching the unfair situation in which she finds herself.
(*The Hunger Games,* Chapter 3)

Yields 4–6 servings

3½ pounds pork shoulder

1½ cups water

1 cup vinegar

1/3 cup soy sauce

2 onions, diced

2 cloves garlic, crushed

2 tablespoons pepper

3 bay leaves

5 sprigs fresh thyme

4 cinnamon sticks

3 tablespoons turbinado or white sugar

Kosher salt to taste

Tips from Your Sponsor

While pork belly is by far the fattiest cut of pork, pork shoulder and butt are close seconds. Thus, don't be surprised if your stew is a bit fatty. However, like chicken skin on fried chicken, this pork fat will make your cooking taste all the more delicious and flavorful.

1. Combine the pork shoulder, water, vinegar, soy sauce, onions, garlic, and pepper together in a stockpot; bring to a boil. Allow to boil for 2–3 minutes.

2. Reduce heat to medium low; add bay leaves, fresh thyme, cinnamon sticks, sugar, and salt. Stir for 10 seconds. Allow the stew to simmer while remaining covered, stirring occasionally, until the meat pulls easily from the bones and the liquid has thickened (about 2 hours).

3. Discard bay leaves and thyme before serving. Serve over rice.

FATHER-DAUGHTER YUCCA FLOWER STALKS AU GRATIN

Katniss and her father spend many happy afternoons gathering roots and plants to feed the family—an act that both ties Katniss to the land and teaches her how to fend for herself. One of the many lessons Mr. Everdeen would have taught Katniss would be to check each yucca stalk for bitterness. (*The Hunger Games*, Chapter 3)

Yields 4 servings

2 cups yucca stalks, peeled and cut into 2" pieces (can be found online or at specialty stores)

3 tablespoons butter

½ cup grated cheese

2 tablespoons sour cream

Tips from Your Sponsor

Not in the mood for this dish? Try making yucca soup! Peel and strip one yucca root, and boil in enough water to remain covered. Meanwhile, in another pan, sauté 2 or 3 yellow onions in 32 ounces of vegetable broth. Add onions and salt and pepper to boiled yucca. Transfer all to a blender; purée. Add cilantro to taste.

1. In a small amount of water, steam yucca stalks for 25–30 minutes, until tender.

2. Arrange in bottom of serving dish.

3. Melt butter in saucepan. Add cheese and sour cream. Stir until blended.

4. Pour over yucca stalks and serve.

The names of many of the characters in *The Hunger Games* showcase the qualities that those characters possess. Katniss, who stays strong in any situation, is named after the Katniss (arrowhead) plant, an incredibly adaptable plant that can survive in temperatures as low as 0°F.
(*The Hunger Games*, Chapter 4)

Yields 4 servings

2 cups arrowhead tubers, washed and scrubbed (found online or in specialty stores)

1 tablespoon butter

1 small onion, chopped

2 celery stalks, chopped

2 carrots, chopped

¼ cup sour cream

1 teaspoon Wild Herb Seasoning

> ### > Wild Herb Seasoning (1 cup)
>
> 1 cup dried greens (cress, purslane, stinging nettle, kudzu)
>
> ¼ cup dried saltwort (can be found in specialty stores or online)
>
> 1 tablespoon dried wild chives
>
> ¼ teaspoon garlic mustard seeds
>
> ¼ teaspoon evening primrose seeds
>
> Blend ingredients in blender or coffee grinder. Sprinkle over your favorite foods.

1. Slice arrowhead tubers. Place into a large saucepan and cover with water. Boil gently about 20–30 minutes, until tender. Drain tubers.

2. In a saucepan over medium heat, melt the butter. Add the onion, celery, and carrots and sauté until tender, about 10 minutes.

3. Add sautéed vegetables, sour cream, and seasonings to cooked tubers. Mix well to combine and serve.

RAGING WILD MUSHROOM RAGOUT

Along with teaching his daughter to recognize wild herbs, Mr. Everdeen would have shown Katniss how to distinguish the poisonous wild mushrooms from the edible ones — an act that clues us into Katniss's good judgment and self-sufficiency. Once Katniss found a crop of edible wild mushrooms, she could make this delicious ragout with very little effort.
(*The Hunger Games*, Chapter 4)

Yields 4–6 servings

1 pound wild mushrooms (such as morels, shiitake, cremini, or oyster)

¼ cup (½ stick) butter

1 leek, cleaned and tender white part sliced

2 cloves garlic, minced

¾ cup heavy cream

Juice of 1 lemon

Kosher salt and freshly ground white pepper to taste

Tips from Your Sponsor

Mushrooms are technically a form of fungi, but their health benefits and delicious taste more than outweigh that ick factor. And mushrooms aren't just good for eating — they also can be used to dye natural fibers such as wool! In fact, before the invention of synthetic dyes, mushrooms were the source of many textile dyes . . . a fact that many of the women in the Seam might find useful for their sewing.

1. Brush mushrooms clean and remove any tough stems. Slice larger mushrooms, halve medium-sized, and leave the small ones whole. Set aside.

2. Melt butter in a large skillet over medium-high heat. Add sliced leek and sauté for 1 minute. Add garlic and cook for another minute. Then add mushrooms. Toss to cook until tender and browned, about 3–4 minutes. Add cream and bring to a boil. Add lemon juice. Season to taste with salt and pepper and serve hot.

LOVELORN PEETA PITA WILDFLOWER POCKETS

Throughout The Hunger Games trilogy, flowers demonstrate that just because something is beautiful doesn't mean that there's no strength underneath, just as with Katniss herself. Sometimes wildflowers were all Katniss had to keep her family fed, but with a little ingenuity, a small bunch of wildflowers can go a long way.
(*The Hunger Games*, Chapter 4 and Chapter 20)

Yields 6 servings

2 cups assorted edible flowers (henbit, wood sorrel, violets, redbud, wild mustard. Before eating, make sure your wildflowers are nontoxic. If unsure, do not eat.)

1 cup mixed salad greens

1 tablespoon lemon juice

1 tablespoon maple syrup

6 pita breads

Tips from Your Sponsor

For an even healthier option, try using whole wheat pitas. Or just eat the wildflower salad and skip the pita altogether!

1. Combine flowers and greens in a large bowl.

2. In a small bowl, mix lemon juice and maple syrup. Pour over salad mixture.

3. Stuff in pita breads and serve.

MRS. EVERDEEN'S RABBIT STEW

Sinking into a depressed stupor after the death of her husband, it is only after Katniss shows up with a snared rabbit—her first successful hunt alone—that Mrs. Everdeen is able to rouse herself out of her funk. Food represents comfort to those in the Seam—as opposed to those in the Capitol who view food as a disposable fact of life.
(*The Hunger Games,* Chapter 4)

Yields 4–6 servings

3 slices bacon

1 (2- to 3-pound) rabbit, cut into pieces

1 cup seasoned flour, see sidebar

4 tablespoons vegetable oil or bacon grease

1 onion, sliced

1 clove garlic, minced

4 sprigs Italian parsley, chopped

1 (8-ounce) can chopped tomatoes, preferably Italian Roma

1 teaspoon dried basil

1 teaspoon dried oregano

¼ cup port wine

Kosher salt and freshly ground pepper to taste

Tips From Your Sponsor

For Seasoned Flour, for every 2 cups of flour combine with 2 tablespoons sea salt, 1 teaspoon pepper, 2 teaspoons dry mustard, 4 teaspoons paprika, 2 teaspoons garlic powder, 1 teaspoon ginger, ½ teaspoon thyme, ½ teaspoon sweet basil, ½ teaspoon dried powdered rosemary, 1 teaspoon onion salt, and 1 teaspoon oregano.

1. Fry bacon in a large skillet until crisp; remove from skillet and set aside. Reserve bacon grease in a small bowl. Dredge pieces of meat in seasoned flour. Sauté in oil or bacon grease over medium-high heat until well browned. Place pieces of meat in a slow cooker.

2. Sauté onion and garlic with reserved bacon grease in a skillet for about 5 minutes over medium heat. Spoon into slow cooker. Add the parsley, tomatoes and their juice, herbs, and port; season with salt and pepper to taste. Cook over low heat for 6–8 hours.

3. Serve hot over rice, noodles, or toasted sourdough bread.

THE EVERDEEN FAMILY'S
DANDELION SALAD OF HOPE

After almost starving to death, a revived Katniss notices a fresh dandelion growing and remembers her father's teachings on edible plants. That a weed ended up feeding an entire family is important: Just because something comes from humble beginnings doesn't mean it can't achieve greatness. Additionally, the color yellow traditionally represents hope, yet another reason this weed is the perfect flower for the situation.
(*The Hunger Games*, Chapter 4)

Yields 4 servings

½ pound torn dandelion greens

½ red onion, chopped

6 grape tomatoes, chopped

1 cup mango halves, chopped

½ cup toasted pine nuts

½ cup fresh mozzarella, shredded

Salt and pepper to taste

Tips from Your Sponsor

Make sure your dandelion greens are young, without any signs of a flower bud. The older your greens, the more bitter the taste! To offset any additional bitterness, try adding a simple balsamic vinegar and olive oil dressing. Or, for a sharper taste, use Gorgonzola instead of mozzarella cheese.

1. In a large bowl, toss together dandelion greens, red onion, grape tomatoes, mango halves, and pine nuts.

2. Sprinkle mozzarella, salt, and pepper on top of salad and serve.

LEMON-SCENTED GREEN PEAS AND ONION MEDLEY

A little bit of flavor goes a long way in this vegetable medley—the perfect side to serve with any entrée. Even the Everdeens with their limited resources would be able to concoct a similarly delicious dish! (*The Hunger Games*, Chapter 5)

Yields 6 servings

3 tablespoons extra-virgin olive oil

2 Vidalia sweet onions, thinly sliced

1 cup shelled fresh peas

2 tablespoons fresh lemon juice

1 tablespoon grated lemon peel

Tips from Your Sponsor

Green peas are a great source of nutrients and vitamins such as vitamin K, which helps maintain bone health. If Katniss or Peeta didn't get enough vitamin K, they'd be no match for the other tributes. For extra protein, add ½ to 1 cup shelled edamame and black beans to this dish!

1. Heat oil in a large nonstick skillet over medium-high heat.

2. Add onions; sauté for one minute. Add peas, lemon juice, and lemon peel. Sauté for 2 minutes to blend flavors. Goes well over jasmine rice.

WILD CREAM OF MUSHROOM SOUP

Katniss is given soup for dinner after she is presented to the adoring public in the Capitol. As Katniss quietly eats her soup, she doesn't realize that many of the ingredients in her dinner are as wild as she is—these mushrooms, onions, and thyme could easily be found back home at her beloved District 12. (*The Hunger Games*, Chapter 6)

Yields 4 servings

1½ pounds fresh mushrooms such as cremini

½ cup (1 stick) butter

5 green onions, chopped

3 cloves garlic, chopped

1 teaspoon fresh lemon juice

1 teaspoon fresh thyme, chopped

Salt and pepper to taste

3 tablespoons all-purpose flour

4 cups vegetable broth

1 cup heavy cream

1 tablespoon apple cider

Tips from Your Sponsor

For the greatest flavor, try a blend of mushrooms in this dish. While shiitake mushrooms are the most popular mushrooms to use for soup, using some porcini and morels as well will give your soup quite a kick! My favorite method is a combination of shiitake and porcini.

1. Brush mushrooms clean. Thinly slice the mushroom caps. Discard the stalks.

2. Melt butter in a large skillet over low heat. Add onions, garlic, lemon, and thyme, stirring for 1 minute, or until the garlic and onions are golden brown. Add the mushrooms, and then salt and pepper to taste. Cook for 4–5 minutes, or until the mushrooms just barely soften. Add flour and stir for 1 minute.

3. Remove from heat. Add the stock, stirring continuously. Return to the heat and bring mixture to a boil, still stirring. Reduce heat and gently simmer for 2 minutes, stirring occasionally.

4. Whisk the heavy cream into the soup, then reheat gently, stirring the whole time. Do not allow the soup to boil. Add cider. Season to taste with more salt and pepper.

SWEET GRAPE AND GORGONZOLA SALAD WITH CANDIED GARLIC

You're able to see just how lavish the meals from the Capitol are in comparison to the meals from District 12 when Katniss describes a delicious side dish with "cheese that melts on your tongue served with sweet blue grapes." What would normally be a plain old side dish to most is worthy of the most luxurious descriptions by Katniss.

(*The Hunger Games*, Chapter 6)

Yields 8 servings

> Dressing:

½ cup aged red wine vinegar

½ cup fresh lemon juice

2 teaspoons sugar

1 tablespoon sea salt

6 cloves garlic

2 small shallots, minced

1½ cups extra-virgin olive oil

2 teaspoons white pepper

> Candied Garlic:

30 cloves garlic

1½ cups water

½ cup sugar

> Salad:

2 cups seedless Concord grapes, sliced

1½ cups Gorgonzola cheese, crumbled

1 cup walnut halves

3 heads romaine lettuce, leaves torn into bite-sized pieces

1. Using an immersion blender, mix together the red wine vinegar, lemon juice, sugar, salt, and 6 cloves garlic. Add shallots and slowly add the olive oil while the immersion blender is on high setting. Season with white pepper and let dressing chill for at least 24 hours before serving.

2. Place the 30 cloves garlic and water in a large pan over high heat. Boil the garlic cloves until they are cooked through but still firm and retaining their shape. By this time the water should be almost completely evaporated.

3. Lower the heat to medium. Add the sugar to the garlic cloves, stirring occasionally. The sugar will begin to caramelize after a few minutes. Now make sure to stir the garlic continuously so it becomes evenly coated with the caramelized sugar. Continue to caramelize the garlic until it is dark golden brown.

4. Grease a baking sheet with oil. Place caramelized garlic onto greased baking sheet and let cool.

5. Put the grapes, Gorgonzola, walnut halves, and candied garlic in a large bowl. Add 1 cup dressing, tossing ingredients. Add romaine lettuce and toss again. Serve.

Tips from Your Sponsor

Can't find Concord grapes? Any purple/blue grape will do. For added flavor, try halving the amount of purple grapes and make up the difference with red grapes. Either way, grapes are great for the heart and may help lower blood pressure.

I'M NOT BITTER GREENS SALAD

The bitterness of the salad mirrors that which Katniss feels when she and Peeta sit down for dinner with their team to discuss strategies for the arena. While that salad uses cherry tomatoes, this salad uses pears to form a satisfying dichotomy between the bitter greens and sweet pears.
(*The Hunger Games*, Chapter 6)

Yields 8–10 servings

> Salad:
5 firm Bosc pears, cored and cut into wedges

5 firm Chojuro or other Asian pears, cored and cut into wedges

2 tablespoons extra-virgin olive oil

1 small head romaine

1 small head chicory

1 small head escarole

1 small head radicchio

1 cup toasted pecans

¼ cup sliced almonds

> Dressing:
1 tablespoon finely chopped shallots

2½ tablespoons cider vinegar

1 teaspoon honey

½ teaspoon sea salt

¼ teaspoon coarse black pepper

1/3 cup extra-virgin olive oil

1. Preheat oven to 400°F.

2. Toss pears in olive oil, then spread in a single layer in a shallow baking pan. Season with salt and pepper. Roast pears, turning over at least twice, until pears are tender and begin to brown, about 25–30 minutes. Cool for 10 minutes.

3. As pears cool, tear romaine, chicory, escarole, and radicchio into bite-sized pieces. Toss greens into a large bowl.

4. In a small bowl, thoroughly whisk together shallots, vinegar, honey, salt, pepper, and oil.

5. Toss greens with dressing. Add roasted pears, pecans, and almonds to salad and serve.

Tips from Your Sponsor

It's not necessary to use all the types of lettuce suggested in this recipe. For an easier mix, just use a bag of baby greens with watercress. And if you can't find Asian pears, try using D'Anjou.

GALE'S BONE-PICKIN' BIG GAME SOUP

Katniss and Gale banded together as hunting allies (and more importantly, as friends) to help each other survive and feed their families. It's likely that Gale—not to mention his mother or Greasy Sae—would find this recipe useful for the meaty bones of their nearly picked-clean wild game. (*The Hunger Games*, Chapter 8)

Yields 8–10 servings

2 pounds meaty soup bones

6 whole cloves

6 allspice berries (whole allspice)

1 teaspoon black peppercorns

2 onions, roughly sliced

2–3 carrots, roughly chopped

1 teaspoon kosher salt

½ cup (1 stick) butter

7 tablespoons all-purpose flour

3½ cups beef stock or consommé

1 (28-ounce) can diced fire-roasted tomatoes

Zest and juice of 1 small lemon

Kosher salt and freshly ground black pepper to taste

Tips from Your Sponsor

This soup takes a while to make, but is well worth the effort. You can ask your local butcher for meaty soup bones, though more and more greenmarkets carry them. Experiment with different kinds of meat to develop your preferred flavor!

1. In a large stockpot, place the soup bones, cloves, allspice, peppercorns, onions, carrots, and 1 teaspoon kosher salt. Fill with 3 quarts of water and bring to a boil. Lower heat to a simmer and cook, uncovered, until meat is tender, 4–6 hours. Do not stir. Allow stock to simmer while meat cools.

2. Remove meaty soup bones from stock. When cool, pick the meat from the bones, dice, and set aside. Place picked bones back into the stock.

3. Bring stock to a boil and cook over high heat until it is reduced to about 1 quart.

4. Strain stock into another bowl or pan and let it cool. Discard spices, vegetables, and bones.

5. In the large pot, melt the butter and stir in the flour to form a roux, a cooked mixture of wheat flour and fat commonly used in Cajun cuisine. Cook over medium heat for about 7–8 minutes to brown. Slowly pour in the beef stock or consommé and stir well to blend with the roux. Add the game stock, diced meat, tomatoes and their juice, and lemon zest and juice. Cook over medium heat until hot. Season to taste with salt and pepper.

KATNISS'S FAVORITE LAMB STEW WITH DRIED PLUMS

Katniss's favorite food from the Capitol is the delicious lamb stew with dried plums. It's no coincidence that this is her favorite dish. Soups and stews are common foods in the Seam, and this healthy and filling dish likely reminded her of the home and family she desperately missed. (*The Hunger Games*, Chapter 9)

Yields 8–10 servings

5 pounds lamb fillet, shoulder or leg, cut into 2" pieces

2 teaspoons salt

½ teaspoon ground black pepper

½ cup all-purpose flour

2 tablespoons olive oil

3 cloves garlic, minced

1 large onion, chopped

½ cup water

4 cups beef stock

2 teaspoons white sugar

3 teaspoons brown sugar

3 cups diced carrots

1 cup diced zucchini

1½ cups diced celery

2 large onions, diced

3 potatoes, cubed

5 cups dried plums

2 teaspoons dried thyme

3 teaspoons chopped fresh rosemary

2 teaspoons chopped fresh basil

1 teaspoon chopped fresh parsley

2 bay leaves

1 cup ginger ale

1. Place lamb, salt, pepper, and flour in a large mixing bowl. Toss to coat meat evenly.

2. Heat olive oil in a large pan and brown the meat, working in batches if you have to.

3. Remove lamb to a side plate. Pour off fat, leaving ¼ cup in the pan. Add the garlic and onion and sauté until the onion becomes golden. Deglaze frying pan with the ½ cup water, taking care to scrape the bottom of the pan to stir up all of the tasty bits of meat and onion. Cook to reduce liquid slightly, then remove from heat.

4. Place the lamb and garlic-onion mixture in a large stockpot. Add beef stock and sugar, stirring until sugars are dissolved. Bring mixture to a boil, cover, and simmer for 1½ hours.

5. Add the vegetables, dried plums, herbs, and ginger ale to the pot. Simmer for 30–45 minutes, or until meat and vegetables pierce easily with a fork.

Tips from Your Sponsor

One of the many great things about this recipe is that it's relatively simple, as long as you aren't daunted by the long list of ingredients. To simplify this recipe even more, you can cook it in a slow cooker. All you have to do is throw all of the ingredients listed above except the flour into the slow cooker on the low setting *at least* 10 hours before you want to eat the stew. About half an hour before you plan to eat, stir in the flour and put the slow cooker on "high." Allow the stew to sit for 5 minutes before serving to allow it to thicken. Ladle into bowls and serve with a hunk of crusty bread.

BROILED JAPANESE KNOTWEED

Katniss has eaten a variety of vegetation in her lifetime. Yet, the fact that she can eat a handful of tree bark during the 74th Hunger Games to ease her hunger showcases how her hard upbringing has enabled her innate survival instinct. The broiled Japanese knotweed used in this recipe is just another kind of foliage Katniss may enjoy with relative ease.
(*The Hunger Games*, Chapter 11)

Yields 6–8 servings

10–12 Japanese knotweed spears, about 6 inches in length (found in specialty stores or online)

1 teaspoon Wild Herb Seasoning (Chapter 3)

2 tablespoons butter, melted

Tips from Your Sponsor

Japanese knotweed tastes surprisingly similar to rhubarb. You should be careful about how much Japanese knotweed you eat, as it is a concentrated source of emodin, a natural laxative.

1. Preheat oven to 350°F. Butter a baking dish that's just big enough to hold the spears.

2. Arrange knotweed spears on bottom of buttered baking dish.

3. Mix herb seasoning with melted butter. Drizzle over knotweed spears.

4. Bake for 10 minutes.

RUE'S ROASTED PARSNIPS

When Rue and Katniss team up and pool their resources, Rue contributes a root vegetable resembling parsnip to their hoard. This root vegetable is symbolic of Rue herself; a small girl who has been over-looked during the games. Fortunately, Katniss, who is familiar with foraged foods, recognizes Rue's true potential, which is what even cooking novices will be able to do with this delicious recipe. (*The Hunger Games*, Chapter 15)

Yields 4 servings

2 pounds of parsnips, peeled and cut into 2" slices

5 teaspoons extra-virgin olive oil

1 tablespoon lemon juice

Kosher salt and freshly ground black pepper to taste

1/3 cup vegetable stock

½ cup (1 stick) unsalted butter, softened

4 teaspoons drained horseradish

1 tablespoon brown sugar

1 tablespoon finely chopped flat-leaf parsley

1 teaspoon fresh rosemary, chopped

1 teaspoon fresh thyme, chopped

½ tablespoon minced chives

1 small garlic clove, minced

Tips from Your Sponsor

Parsnip is a root vegetable closely related to the carrot. It can be cooked and used much like carrots, and is sweeter in taste. These vegetables are especially delicious when pan fried in a ½ cup of butter with ¼ cup of flour and a teaspoon of sea salt.

1. Preheat oven to 400°F. In a large roasting pan with sides no more than 2" high, toss the parsnips with the olive oil, lemon juice, and salt and pepper to taste. Add the stock, and cover the pan with aluminum foil.

2. Roast parsnips, stirring once or twice, until tender and the stock has evaporated or been absorbed, about 20–45 minutes. Check often to avoid mushiness.

3. Combine the softened butter with the horseradish, brown sugar, parsley, rosemary, thyme, chives, and garlic. Season with salt and pepper. Toss the warm parsnips with the herb butter and serve.

SWEET AND SOUR CRANAPPLE SALAD

Considering the amount of berries and nuts Rue has gathered, this is another possible salad Rue and Katniss could make once they join forces. Like Katniss's personality, this salad with its collection of fruits and nuts is both sweet and sour.
(*The Hunger Games*, Chapter 15)

Yields 8 servings

2 cups wild cranberries (if available, otherwise frozen cultivated cranberries may be used as long as they are thawed an hour before cooking)

1 cup maple syrup, or to taste

1 stalk celery, chopped

2 medium apples, chopped

¼ cup nuts, chopped

Tips from Your Sponsor

Research studies show that cranberries and blueberries both contain compounds that prevent bacteria from adhering to the bladder walls, thus preventing bladder infections (cystitis). They also contain arbutin, which is both an antibiotic and a diuretic.

1. Put cranberries and maple syrup in small saucepan.

2. Bring to a gentle boil and continue to cook about 15–20 minutes, until berries have popped and start to thicken.

3. Remove from heat and add remaining ingredients. Chill 1 hour before serving.

RUE AND KATNISS'S STIR-FRIED MILKWEED BUDS, FLOWERS, AND PODS

Katniss and Rue show their self-sufficiency by gathering roots and berries to stay alive. If they'd only had a little bit of butter, they could have made this delicious dish.
(*The Hunger Games*, Chapter 16)

Yields 6–8 servings

2 tablespoons butter (or vegetable oil)

1 medium onion, chopped

2–3 carrots, chopped

2 cups milkweed buds, flowers, and pods, heated on a skillet on low for five minutes

Tips from Your Sponsor

Milkweed buds look just like little green peas when cooked and make a nice addition to potato dishes.

1. Melt butter in saucepan over medium heat.

2. Sauté onions and carrots in melted butter about 5 minutes.

3. Add milkweed buds, flowers, and pods to onions and carrots.

4. Reduce heat and simmer for 5–10 minutes.

5. Serve as a side dish or with rice.

FRESH FROM THE CAREERS' PACKS: SUPER HEALTHY DRIED FRUIT QUINOA SALAD

While Katniss is able to find and gather her own fresh food, the Careers can only survive on the premade, preserved snacks that they grabbed when they first entered the arena. This juxtaposition gives you a good idea of who is more likely to survive. If only she had some quinoa, Katniss could blend it with the stolen fruit to make the incredibly healthy (not to mention filling) quinoa salad below. (*The Hunger Games*, Chapter 18)

Yields 6–8 servings

1 ½ cups quinoa (rinsed well)

½ teaspoon table salt

3 ½ cups water

¼ cup scallions, chopped

1 cup celery, chopped

½ cup dried cranberries

½ cup dried cherries

1 teaspoon hot sauce

½ teaspoon garlic powder

1 tablespoon vegetable oil

2 tablespoons lemon juice

2 tablespoons sesame oil

1/3 cup fresh cilantro, chopped

½ cup toasted almonds, chopped

¼ cup sunflower seeds (optional)

Tips from Your Sponsor

Try a variety of nuts and seeds instead of almonds and sunflower seeds. Toasted pecans and pumpkin seeds add an unusual flavor. Add grilled chicken strips for further protein, or raisins for extra sweetness.

1. Bring quinoa, salt, and water to boil in a saucepan. Reduce heat to medium low and simmer until quinoa is tender, about 30 minutes. Drain quinoa and transfer it to a larger bowl. Allow to cool for 15 minutes.

2. Stir into the quinoa the scallions, celery, dried fruit, hot sauce, garlic powder, vegetable oil, lemon juice, and sesame oil. Let stand at room temperature for at least 1 hour so flavors can blend.

3. Add the cilantro, almonds, and sunflower seeds and serve.

ROOT SOUP FOR PEETA

While huddling in their secret cave, Katniss puts together this soup of roots and groosling in her attempt to warm the suffering Peeta. Soup represents comfort and healing and here, not only does this soup heal Peeta physically, it helps mend Katniss and Peeta's relationship, allowing them to work together to survive the Hunger Games. Don't hesitate to make this soup for yourself if you're not feeling well. (*The Hunger Games*, Chapter 20)

Yields 8–10 servings

1 quart water

2 cups stinging nettle greens, chopped

4–6 evening primrose roots, peeled and chopped

4–6 Jerusalem artichoke tubers, chopped

1 cup chopped roots (combination of dandelion roots, burdock roots, yellow dock roots, or other roots, depending on what's available)

½ cup rock tripe, broken up into small pieces

2 tablespoons vegetable oil or butter

1 medium onion, chopped

2 celery stalks, chopped

3 carrots, chopped

Field garlic or wild onion tops, chopped

1 dried cayenne or chili pepper

½ teaspoon evening primrose seeds

Salt and pepper, to taste

1. Heat water to boiling in a medium-sized soup pot.

2. Add nettles and let cook for 2 minutes.

3. Add evening primrose roots, Jerusalem artichokes, chopped roots, and rock tripe.

4. Heat oil or butter in saucepan and sauté onions, celery, and carrots.

5. Add to soup pot, along with field garlic or onion tops, cayenne or chili pepper, and evening primrose seeds. Cook on medium-low heat for at least 30 minutes. Season with salt and pepper to taste.

Tips from Your Sponsor

Herbs that are used to cleanse the liver are called hepatic herbs. They help by triggering the flow of bile. This group of herbs includes dandelion root, burdock root, and yellow dock root. Their roots grow deep into the ground, making them rich in minerals and useful as a liver tonic.

GREASY SAE'S BLACK BEAN PUMPKIN SOUP

Before Katniss is forced to go on the Victory Tour, she visits Greasy Sae's stall in the Hob. There she eats a thick soup of gourd and beans in an attempt to keep the familiarity of home with her as she mentally prepares herself to leave.
(*Catching Fire*, Chapter 1)

Yields 6–8 servings

4 tablespoons extra-virgin olive oil

2 medium yellow onions, finely chopped

4 cups vegetable stock

2 (15-ounce) cans black beans, drained

2 (15-ounce) cans pumpkin purée

1 cup heavy cream

1 tablespoon curry powder

1 tablespoon garlic salt

1½ teaspoons ground cumin

½ teaspoon cayenne pepper

½ teaspoon hot sauce

Sea salt

½ cup green onions, chopped for garnish

Tips from Your Sponsor

The great thing about this soup is that you can always add and substitute ingredients. Feel free to add frozen corn or some chopped, boiled potatoes to this soup. Not a fan of spice? Then forgo the hot sauce in place of a teaspoon of cinnamon.

1. Heat a large stockpot over medium-high heat. Add olive oil. When oil is hot, add yellow onions. Sauté onions for 7 minutes. Stir in stock, beans, and pumpkin purée until ingredients are fully mixed. Bring soup to a boil and reduce heat to medium-low.

2. Add cream, curry powder, garlic salt, cumin, cayenne pepper, and hot sauce. Add salt to taste. Simmer for 7 minutes.

3. Adjust seasonings to fit personal taste. Serve garnished with chopped green onions.

CHILLED RASPBERRY AND CHERRY SOUP

As Katniss learns, not all soups need to be warm to be delicious, and sometimes even the most well-meaning comfort can leave you feeling cold. Along with the many options at the banquet, this chilled sweet soup works as either an appetizer or a dessert to any meal.
(*Catching Fire*, Chapter 6)

Yields 6 servings

20 ounces frozen raspberries, thawed

20 ounces frozen cherries, thawed

1½ cups water

½ cup white wine, chilled

1½ cups cranberry juice

½ cup sugar

2 teaspoons ground cinnamon

2 teaspoons ground cloves

3 tablespoons lemon juice

1 (8-ounce) container cherry yogurt

1 (8-ounce) container vanilla yogurt

1 cup fresh raspberries

½ cup sour cream

Tips from Your Sponsor

This is a very sweet soup. To cut down on sweetness, use plain yogurt instead of vanilla, and be sure to add a heaping spoonful of sour cream to cut down on the soup's sugary taste.

1. In a blender, purée raspberries and cherries with water and wine. Transfer to a large saucepan. Add cranberry juice, sugar, cinnamon, and cloves. Bring to boil over medium heat.

2. Remove from heat. Strain and allow to cool. Whisk in lemon juice and both yogurts. Refrigerate.

3. To serve, pour into small bowls and top with fresh raspberries and a dollop of sour cream.

CAPITOL CREAM OF PUMPKIN SOUP WITH SLIVERED NUTS AND CINNAMON CROUTONS

This creamy concoction is one of the many soups offered at the banquet held in Katniss and Peeta's honor, and it's the first thing Katniss tries after she realizes that her performance has been unable to halt the looming protests. That she begins her time at the banquet with this elegant soup consisting of such modest ingredients foreshadows the side which Katniss must—and will—join.
(*Catching Fire*, Chapter 6)

Yields 6–8 servings

3 tablespoons butter, softened

3 tablespoons brown sugar

½ teaspoon ground cinnamon

4 slices whole wheat bread

1 cup chopped onion

2 tablespoons butter, melted

2 (14.5-ounce) cans chicken broth

1 (15-ounce) can pumpkin purée

½ cup brown sugar

¼ teaspoon salt

¼ teaspoon ground cinnamon

¼ teaspoon ground ginger

½ teaspoon pumpkin pie spice

¼ teaspoon nutmeg

¼ teaspoon ground black pepper

1 cup heavy whipping cream

½ cup roasted pumpkin seeds

½ cup slivered almonds

Tips from Your Sponsor

One gram of pumpkin-seed protein contains as much tryptophan as a glass of milk! Pumpkin *and* its seeds are also full of iron, potassium, fiber, and antioxidants.

1. Preheat oven to 400°F. Combine butter, brown sugar, and cinnamon. Spread butter mixture evenly over one side of each bread slice. Place bread, buttered side up, on a baking sheet. Bake for 8 minutes, or until bread is crisp and topping bubbles. Remove from oven and cut each slice of bread into 8 squares for croutons.

2. In a medium saucepan, sauté onion in butter until tender. Add 1 can chicken broth; stir well. Bring to boil, cover, reduce heat, and simmer for 10 minutes. Remove from heat and let cool for 5 minutes.

3. Transfer broth mixture into a blender or processor. Process until smooth.

4. Return mixture to saucepan. Add remaining can of broth, pumpkin purée, brown sugar, salt, cinnamon, ginger, pumpkin pie spice, nutmeg, and pepper. Stir well. Bring to boil; cover, reduce heat, and simmer 15 minutes, stirring occasionally.

5. Stir in whipping cream and heat through, but do not boil. Ladle into individual soup bowls. Top each serving with cinnamon croutons, roasted pumpkin seeds, and slivered almonds.

Katniss describes this soup as "tasting like springtime," a season that represents hope, fertility, and rebellion after the long, cold winter of the Capitol's reign. The vegetables in this soup are indeed in season in the spring.
(*Catching Fire*, Chapter 6)

Yields 6–8 servings

2 large leeks (white and green parts only), thinly sliced

2 celery ribs, chopped

2 large carrots, chopped

2 garlic cloves, finely chopped

1 large thyme sprig

1 large oregano sprig

1 large rosemary sprig

2 tablespoons extra-virgin olive oil

4 teaspoons salt

2 teaspoons pepper

½ pound Yukon Gold or fingerling potatoes, peeled and cut into ½" pieces

2 cups water

6 cups chicken or vegetable stock

½ cup green peas

½ cup white beans

½ cup garbanzo beans

½ cup fava beans

½ pound fresh spinach leaves, stems finely chopped and leaves coarsely chopped

1. In a 6-quart heavy pot over medium heat, cook leeks, celery, carrots, garlic, thyme, oregano, and rosemary in oil with 1 teaspoon of the salt and 1 teaspoon of the pepper, stirring occasionally until vegetables brown.

2. Add potatoes with another teaspoon of salt and the remaining teaspoon of pepper. Cook, stirring occasionally, until potatoes begin to soften, about 5–7 minutes. Add water and chicken or vegetable stock and bring to a boil, stirring and scraping up brown bits from the bottom of the pan.

3. Stir in green peas, white beans, garbanzo beans, fava beans, spinach, and the remaining 2 teaspoons of salt. Cook uncovered until vegetables are tender, about 10 minutes.

4. Before serving, discard thyme, oregano, and rosemary sprigs.

Tips from Your Sponsor

In ancient Greece and Rome, beans were used for voting. White beans were used to cast a "yes" vote, black beans for "no." This would have been problematic for followers of the Greek philosopher Pythagoras, as he forbade his followers from eating, or even touching, any beans.

SURVIVAL OF THE FITTEST: QUINOA AND BLACK BEAN SALAD FOR BONNIE AND TWILL

For their journey into the legendary District 13, Katniss is only able to give Bonnie and Twill grain and dried beans, but these simple ingredients turn into something lifesaving and inspiring—just like Bonnie and Twill.
(*Catching Fire*, Chapter 10)

Yields 4–6 servings

> Salad:

1½ cups quinoa

3 cups water

2 cups cooked black beans

1½ tablespoons red-wine vinegar

Kosher salt and ground black pepper to taste

2 cups cooked corn

½ cup scallions, chopped

1 cup red bell pepper, chopped

½ cup fresh coriander, chopped

Pinch of cayenne pepper

½ cup cherry tomatoes, halved

2 fresh avocados, peeled, pitted, and chopped

> Dressing:

4 tablespoons fresh lime juice

2 tablespoons fresh lemon juice

2 teaspoons kosher salt

1 teaspoon ground cumin

¼ cup extra-virgin olive oil

1. In a bowl, wash quinoa thoroughly until water runs clear. Drain.

2. Boil lightly salted water in a large saucepan, add quinoa, and cook for 15 minutes. Drain quinoa and rinse under cold water. Steam quinoa until fluffy and dry, about 15 minutes.

3. While quinoa cooks, toss beans with vinegar and kosher salt and black pepper to taste.

4. Transfer quinoa to a large bowl and let cool. Add beans, corn, scallions, red bell peppers, and coriander. Toss with cayenne pepper. Top with cherry tomatoes and avocado.

5. For dressing: Using a small bowl, whisk together lime juice, lemon juice, pink salt, ground cumin, and olive oil, whisking continuously. Drizzle dressing over salad and toss with salt and pepper to taste. Serve at room temperature.

Tips from Your Sponsor

The trick to good quinoa is steaming it, as boiling quinoa does not produce the light and fluffy texture so many of us have come to love.

This soup is best served cold, which is how Katniss feels when she's put on the train to the Capitol to participate in yet another Hunger Games. The hot sauce and cumin in this recipe give this nutritious dish an extra kick, which Katniss will need to fight her own way out of another arena. (*Catching Fire*, Chapter 14)

Yields 4–6 servings

2 pounds ripe tomatoes

1 large cucumber, chopped

1 green bell pepper, chopped

2 cloves crushed garlic

1 tablespoon finely chopped black olives

1/3 cup rice vinegar

1/3 cup extra-virgin olive oil

1 tablespoon tomato paste

Kosher salt and fresh cracked pepper to taste

1 tablespoon fresh cilantro, chopped

1 tablespoon ground cumin

2 teaspoons hot sauce

3 cups water, chilled

1 onion, chopped

1 green bell pepper, diced

2 green onions, chopped

1 large cucumber, chopped

1 cup croutons (optional)

1. Bring a large pot of water to a boil.

2. Using a sharp knife, score a cross in the base of each tomato. Drop tomatoes into boiling water for 1 minute, plunge into cold water, drain, and peel away the skin. Chop the flesh so finely that it is almost a purée.

3. In a large bowl, mix together the tomatoes, 1 chopped onion, 1 chopped green pepper, 1 chopped cucumber, garlic, olives, vinegar, olive oil, and tomato paste, and season with salt and pepper to taste. Mix in fresh cilantro, ground cumin, and hot sauce. Cover and refrigerate for at least 3 hours.

4. Before serving, add 2–3 cups of chilled water to thin the soup to your taste. Serve the soup chilled, allowing guests to top soup with chopped green bell pepper, green onions, cucumber, and croutons to their taste.

Tips from Your Sponsor

There's lots of room for variation with this gazpacho recipe. Not a fan of tomato? Reduce recipe to 1½ pounds tomatoes and bulk up on vegetables (perhaps adding some celery or more bell peppers to the soup). Feel free to experiment with spices and hot sauce.

DISTRICT 13'S MASHED TURNIPS

In District 13 what you see is what you get, and the food eaten in this District represents that stark mentality. So when Katniss sees her vegetable of the day is mashed turnips, that's exactly what it is. Luckily the butter and cream in this recipe adds for some pleasant taste to what could be an unpleasant dish.

(*Mockingjay*, Chapter 3)

Yields 8–10 servings

8 large turnips

½ cup heavy cream

¼ cup (½ stick) unsalted butter

Kosher salt to taste

Freshly ground black pepper to taste

Tips from Your Sponsor

This is a low-carb variation of mashed potatoes. Turnips possess a high water content, so if your mashed turnips turn runny, try reducing the amount of cream added and return turnips to the pot to cook out the excess water.

1. Peel, wash, and quarter turnips.

2. In a large pot, boil turnips for 45 minutes or until tender. Strain and rinsed the cooked turnips.

3. Place turnips in a large bowl and use fork to break them into smaller bits. Mix in cream and butter and blend to desired consistency. Add salt and pepper to taste.

WILD DOG OPTIONAL: PORK AND RHUBARB STEW

We really get to know Greasy Sae when we're told that she can make a wild dog and rhubarb stew. This imaginative dish displays her ability to use anything she can in a meal. Greasy Sae is a survivor who is able to fit in anywhere. That said, it's likely that her stews would be more than palatable if she used pork instead of wild dog!
(*Mockingjay*, Chapter 4)

Yields 8 servings

2 tablespoons extra-virgin olive oil

1 pound ground pork

1 pound fresh hot Italian pork sausage, casing removed

2 large onions, chopped

4 cloves garlic, minced

4 cups chicken broth

1½ pounds rhubarb, cut into 1" pieces

¼ cup chopped fresh basil leaves

1 teaspoon dried oregano

2 (14.5-ounce) cans diced tomatoes seasoned with Italian herbs

1 (16-ounce) can white kidney beans, rinsed and drained

2 cups cauliflower

½ cup green bell peppers, chopped

½ cup red bell peppers, chopped

1 teaspoon crushed red pepper flakes

1 (6-ounce) package fresh kale, washed

1 cup fresh Parmesan cheese, grated

1. Heat oil in a large saucepan over medium-high heat. Add ground pork, sausage, and onions. Cook until meats are browned, constantly stirring. Add garlic and sauté for 1 minute.

2. Mix in broth, rhubarb, basil, oregano, tomatoes, and kidney beans. Bring mixture to a boil. Cover and cook over low heat for 15 minutes, stirring every few minutes. Stir in cauliflower and bell peppers. Let stew simmer for another 5 minutes. Simmer until stew reaches desired consistency. Stir in red pepper flakes.

3. Add kale and cook just until kale looks like it might wilt, stirring occasionally. Remove from heat and stir in ½ cup cheese.

4. Ladle stew into small bowls and top with more cheese.

Tips from Your Sponsor

Lacking kale? You can substitute fresh spinach leaves, but be careful—spinach tends to wilt much more easily than kale and doesn't hold up as well as leftovers.

BLACK BEAN AND PARSNIP SOUP

This soup is black and heated, which is exactly how Katniss feels when eating it after witnessing the torture of Flavius, Venia, and Octavia for "stealing food."
(*Mockingjay*, Chapter 4)

Yields 6–8 servings

1½ tablespoons extra-virgin olive oil

2 medium yellow onions, diced

Kosher salt to taste

3 cloves of garlic, diced

Freshly ground black pepper to taste

1½ teaspoons cumin

1 teaspoon coriander

1 teaspoon freshly ground black pepper

2 quarts chicken or vegetable stock (low sodium)

4 (15-ounce) cans black beans (plain, unsalted), rinsed and drained

2 large parsnips, peeled and cubed

2 limes, sliced for garnish

4 cups plain yogurt or sour cream

1. In a large stockpot or soup pot, heat the olive oil over medium heat. Add the onions and a few pinches of salt. Make sure the oil is hot enough that you can hear the onions sizzle when you add them. Cook until onions are slightly browned, about 8 minutes.

2. Add in the garlic and let it sauté with the onions for another 2 minutes.

3. Add the cumin, coriander, and pepper and stir throughout the onions. Allow the spices to warm up for about 30 seconds. The aroma will fill the kitchen.

4. Add in the stock, black beans, and parsnips. Over high heat, bring the soup to a rolling boil.

5. Turn heat to medium low and allow the soup to simmer for 15 minutes so the parsnips can soften and cook. Taste the soup for seasoning and conservatively add salt and pepper if needed.

6. Turn the heat to its lowest setting. Using a slotted spoon, remove 3 cups of the parsnips, beans, and onions. Set aside.

7. Using an immersion blender, blend the remaining parsnips, beans, and onions in the pot. The soup will become thick and creamy. Don't worry about blending every last bit of the vegetables, but make sure your soup has a fairly thick consistency. If you don't have an immersion blender, you can use an upright blender or food processor, adding the soup in small batches.

8. Return the reserved parsnips, beans, and onions to the soup. Do one last taste test to check the seasoning. Add salt, pepper, or small amounts of cumin or coriander to taste. Remember, you can always add more, but you can't take them out.

9. Serve your soup with a garnish of sliced lime, a spoonful of yogurt or sour cream, and a drizzle of lime juice.

Tips from Your Sponsor

This recipe is both filling and delicious. If you can't find parsnips, feel free to substitute carrots, as they're part of the same family.

GREASY SAE'S FISH AND OKRA STEW

The sliminess of this stew symbolizes Katniss's feelings regarding being used as President Coin's "Mockingjay." While Katniss realizes the necessity of the symbol, she certainly doesn't trust the rebellion. This recipe offers tips on how to rid your stew of this slimy problem while still serving a delicious and spicy meal. (*Mockingjay*, Chapter 5)

Yields 6 servings

> Fish Seasoning:

1 tablespoon paprika

1 tablespoon garlic salt

1 tablespoon dried onion

1 teaspoon ground ginger

1 teaspoon dried mustard

1 tablespoon cayenne

2 teaspoons oregano

½ teaspoon black pepper

½ teaspoon white pepper

> Stew:

¼ cup vegetable oil

2 pounds okra, sliced ½" thick

Sea salt and freshly ground black pepper to taste

2 teaspoons cayenne

2 cups yellow onions, chopped

1 cup celery, chopped

1 cup green bell peppers, chopped

1 cup red bell peppers, chopped

¼ cup fresh parsley, chopped

2 tablespoons chopped garlic

1 pound snapper, diced

6 cups fish stock

2 tablespoons Worcestershire sauce

1 tablespoon hot sauce

1. In a small bowl, combine all the ingredients for the fish seasoning. Set aside.

2. In a large stockpot, heat oil over medium heat. Once oil is hot, add okra, followed by salt and 1 teaspoon cayenne. Stir the okra constantly for 25 minutes, or until most of the slime disappears. Add onions, celery, and bell peppers. Stir in parsley, salt, and the remaining teaspoon of cayenne.

3. Stirring often, continue cooking until the okra and other vegetables are soft and any possible sliminess has completely disappeared. Stir in the garlic.

4. Season the diced snapper with the fish seasoning, thoroughly rubbing the seasoning into the fish. Add seasoned fish to vegetables and cook for 2 minutes. Add the fish stock. Bring to a boil and then reduce to a simmer. Simmer for 20 minutes. Add Worcestershire sauce and hot sauce. Serve over wild rice.

Tips from Your Sponsor

When adding the onions, celery, and bell peppers, allow them to stick to the bottom of the pan, then scrape the bottom with a spoon. This allows some of the natural sugars to caramelize, adding a great deal of flavor to your stew.

Venison is one of the foods Katniss and Gale (and sometimes Finnick) contribute to District 13 once the heroes are allowed to hunt. Like the deer used in this recipe, Katniss used to feel free in the woods, but is now cornered and caged in the controlling District 13.
(*Mockingjay*, Chapter 9)

Yields 6–8 servings

3 pounds venison stew meat (2" cubes)

4 tablespoons olive oil

6 cups beef bouillon

2 envelopes peppercorn gravy mix

2 teaspoons oregano

1 bay leaf

2 cloves garlic, minced

2 cups fresh pearl onions

4 potatoes

6 carrots

1 loaf rustic bread

Tips from Your Sponsor

For an extra-fun dinner dish, try serving this dish in a sourdough bread bowl. That way, you can not only fill up on this hearty stew, but on the actual bowl it comes in!

1. Brown venison in oil in a large Dutch oven. Combine beef bouillon, gravy mix, oregano, bay leaf, garlic, and onions. Bring to a boil, cover, and reduce heat. Simmer for 1 hour.

2. Peel and cut up potatoes and carrots. Add to stew and simmer for another 30 minutes or until vegetables are fork tender.

3. Remove bay leaf. Serve stew in bowls with rustic bread on the side to sop up all the broth.

DISTRICT 13'S REJUVENATING BEEF STEW

Katniss recognizes the rejuvenating effects of a good meal when the refugees and citizens of District 13 eat a filling dinner for the first time in years. Hopefully this dish will have a similar effect at your dinner table.
(*Mockingjay*, Chapter 17)

Yields 8 servings

2 pounds sirloin steak, trimmed and cut into ¾" cubes

2 tablespoons vegetable oil

1 pound red potatoes, cubed

1 cup beef broth

1 cup water

1 tablespoon Worcestershire sauce

2 cloves garlic, peeled

2 bay leaves

1 yellow onion, sliced

1 teaspoon kosher salt

1 teaspoon white sugar

1 teaspoon brown sugar

½ teaspoon freshly ground pepper

1 teaspoon lemon juice

1 teaspoon paprika

1 teaspoon cayenne pepper

1 teaspoon oregano

1 teaspoon ground allspice

3 large carrots, sliced

3 ribs celery, chopped

3 tablespoons butter

1 medium turnip, peeled

¼ cup water

2 tablespoons cornstarch

1. In a large skillet, brown meat in hot oil.

2. In a pot, boil potatoes until soft. Drain and set aside.

3. In a large pot, combine browned steak, beef broth, water, Worcestershire sauce, garlic, bay leaves, onion, salt, sugars, pepper, lemon juice, paprika, cayenne pepper, oregano, and allspice. Cover and simmer for 90 minutes.

4. Remove bay leaves and garlic cloves. Add cooked potatoes, carrots, and celery. Cover and cook for 45 minutes. Remove 2 cups hot liquid to thicken gravy.

5. In a medium-sized skillet, melt butter. Sauté turnips in butter until crusty and brown. Add turnips to stew.

6. In a separate bowl, mix ¼ cup water and cornstarch until smooth. Mix with a little of the reserved hot liquid and return mixture to pot. Stir and cook until bubbly.

7. Ladle into bowls to serve.

Tips from Your Sponsor

For extra spice, try adding garlic salt or a packet of dry onion soup to taste.

PEA SOUP FOR YOUR SORROWS

After a full day of shooting Propos for the rebellion, an exhausted Katniss helps herself to an extra-large portion of pea soup. Sometimes, all you can do when feeling down is eat a bowl of warm soup and hope for a better tomorrow . . . a tomorrow Katniss fights for. The fact that she's allowed to take an extra-large portion of anything in District 13 is indicative of her importance to the rebellion. (*Mockingjay*, Chapter 9)

Yields 5 servings

16 ounces dried split peas

2 medium potatoes, peeled and diced

2 cups diced carrots

½ cup diced celery

2 medium onions, chopped

2 garlic cloves, minced

2 teaspoons salt

2 teaspoons pepper

5 cups chicken or vegetable stock

2 cups water

3 cups frozen peas

1 cup milk

Tips from Your Sponsor

There are infinite variations to this basic pea soup recipe. For the meat eaters in your District, try adding 2 cups fully cooked ham or ½ pound of crisp bacon to the soup just before serving. If you do use bacon, fry it before you continue with the rest of the recipe and then, for an extra kick, sauté the vegetables in the bacon grease before adding them to the slow cooker. If you're a vegan, just skip adding the milk.

1. In a slow cooker, layer all the ingredients but the frozen peas and milk in the order listed. Cover and cook on high for 5–6 hours or until the vegetables are tender.

2. Add the frozen peas and cook for 1 hour, stirring occasionally.

3. Stir in milk and heat through for 15 minutes before serving.

CHAPTER 4

HUMBLE BEGINNINGS

Katniss, Peeta, and Gale each follow the archetypal tale of the hero: They come from very humble beginnings only to be reborn as both the symbols and leaders of the rebellion. And just as these seemingly ordinary characters are revolutionized into heroes, the simple ingredients used in the recipes in this chapter are transformed into small, rich bundles worthy of these brave characters. Indeed, while these dishes are small, their palatable taste packs a powerful bite. As Katniss learns time and time again, appearances can be deceiving and size isn't everything.

PINK MASHED POTATOES WITH EVENING PRIMROSE ROOTS

Katniss's beloved sister Prim is named after the primrose flower. This beautiful flower may appear delicate, but its root is quite hardy. Like her namesake, Prim has a gentle exterior that hides a tough, sturdy soul. After all, it's Prim who keeps her and her mother alive during Katniss's long absences at the Hunger Games.
(*The Hunger Games*, Chapter 1)

Yields 4–6 servings

3 medium-sized potatoes, chopped

4 evening primrose roots, scraped and chopped

1 tablespoon dried Wild Herb Seasoning (Chapter 3)

½ teaspoon evening primrose seeds

½ teaspoon celery seeds

Salt and pepper, to taste

½ cup sour cream

2 tablespoons butter

Tips from Your Sponsor

Evening primrose roots, when cooked, take on a pinkish hue, tinting regular potatoes with their color. The roots have a potent flavor that are tempered (but not masked) by the potatoes.

1. Steam-cook the potatoes, evening primrose roots, herb seasoning, primrose seeds, and celery seeds for about 20 minutes.

2. Put in a large bowl and add remaining ingredients. Mash with a fork or potato masher, adding broth from cooking to desired thickness.

PRIM'S BASIL-WRAPPED GOAT CHEESE BALLS

One of the very first mentions of food in The Hunger Games trilogy comes in the form of a gift from Prim. On Reaping Day, Prim presents her beloved big sister with a gift—goat cheese wrapped in basil leaves. Historically, goats represent sacrifice and giving, and when Prim gives Katniss this goat cheese she foreshadows the many sacrifices the Everdeen family will be forced to make when Katniss volunteers to take Prim's place in the Hunger Games.
(*The Hunger Games*, Chapter 1)

Yields 25 servings

5 ounces goat cheese, at room temperature

4 tablespoons extra-virgin olive oil

2 teaspoons fresh lemon juice

Pinch of sea salt

2 teaspoons freshly ground black pepper

25 large basil leaves

Extra-virgin olive oil to taste

Tips from Your Sponsor

Yes, it's true, goat cheese comes from milking a goat. While this might sound gross, goat's milk has much more in common with human milk than cow's milk does. In fact, in most parts of the world other than the West, goat's milk is the norm!

1. In a small bowl, stir together the goat cheese, olive oil, and lemon juice. Add salt and pepper to taste.

2. Place a spoonful of cheese mixture onto each basil leaf. Drizzle with olive oil and serve.

PINE NEEDLE TEA

It was tea such as this that kept Katniss and her family alive after Mr. Everdeen's death. When Katniss first concocted this tea, thus acknowledging Katniss's survival skills, her understanding was faint and watered-down, but over time she learns how to live off the land and, along with her recipes, the lives of those closest to her improve substantially.
(*The Hunger Games*, Chapter 2)

Yields 4 servings

3–5 clusters of pine needles

1 quart boiling water

Juice of 1 lemon

Maple syrup, to taste

Tips from Your Sponsor

The longer you steep pine needle tea, the stronger it becomes, making it more of a medicine than a tea. Drink the tea as a cold or flu remedy or to boost the immune system.

1. Using kitchen scissors, snip needles into pieces 1"–2" long.

2. Pour boiling water over needles. Add lemon juice.

3. Cover and let steep 5 minutes.

4. Strain needles out of tea.

5. Sweeten to taste with maple syrup and serve.

PRIM'S GOAT CHEESE TRUFFLES

When selling her wares in the Hob, little Prim sets aside a couple of her goat cheese balls for Mr. Mellark. He, in turn, would give her large portions of his bread. Such exchanges foreshadow how the survival of the Everdeen and Mellark families will become even more closely intertwined as The Hunger Games trilogy continues. These goat cheese truffles are just the kind of treat Mr. Mellark would whip up at home—and perhaps sell to the wealthier members of District 12.
(*The Hunger Games*, Chapter 3)

Yields 24 servings

¼ cup fresh basil, chopped

¼ cup fresh thyme, chopped

¼ cup fresh oregano, chopped

1½ cups goat cheese

1 cup cream cheese, softened

4 green onions, chopped

1 teaspoon fresh ground pepper

¼ cup roasted almonds, chopped (optional)

4 teaspoons paprika (optional)

Tips from Your Sponsor

Goat cheese is one of the easiest cheeses to make. In its simplest form, goat cheese is made by warming goat's milk, allowing it to curdle, and then draining and pressing the curds. Cooks all over the world make goat cheese by wrapping the curds in cheesecloth and hanging it in a warm kitchen for several days to drain and cure.

1. In a small bowl, combine the basil, thyme, and oregano.

2. In a slightly larger bowl, mix the goat cheese, cream cheese, green onions, pepper, and 4–5 tablespoons of the herb mixture until smooth. Portion the cheese mixture into balls the size of 2 tablespoons, rolling them in the palm of your hands. It helps if your hands are moist.

3. Roll cheese balls in chopped nuts or the rest of the herb mixture, or sift paprika over them. Serve with toothpicks.

PRIM'S "GETTING BY" GOAT CHEESE SPREAD

After Katniss offers herself up in place of Prim in the reaping, she advises Prim that the family can survive without her by selling Prim's goat milk and cheese in the Hob. Katniss says this not only to pass this information on to Prim, but also to remind Prim that she is capable of taking care of the family—subsequently predicting Prim's work as a healer later on in the series.
(*The Hunger Games*, Chapter 3)

Yields 16 servings

2½ cups crumbled goat cheese, room temperature

2 tablespoons whole milk

2 teaspoons cumin powder

1 teaspoon fresh dill, chopped

½ teaspoon freshly ground black pepper

2 garlic cloves, pressed

¼ cup extra-virgin olive oil

20 mint leaves, thinly sliced

30 whole wheat crackers

Tips from Your Sponsor

For an added kick, try mixing ⅓ to ½ cup chopped sun-dried tomatoes or 2 teaspoons grated lemon peel in with the goat cheese mix and serve with sliced baguettes.

1. Mix goat cheese, milk, cumin powder, fresh dill, black pepper, and garlic in a small bowl until smooth. Cover and chill for at least 24 hours.

2. Transfer chilled spread to a small bowl. Drizzle with olive oil and garnish with mint leaves. Serve with crackers.

CLOVER-MINT TEA

Though small, mint proved its might to Katniss in those first dark days after her father's death when she would often mix mint leaves with hot water in an attempt to fill her aching stomach. Meanwhile, the very greenness of the mint suggests life and renewal, which is what this mint reminds Katniss about.
(*The Hunger Games*, Chapter 2)

Yields 2 servings

2 cups boiling water
1 tablespoon fresh red clover flowers
2 tablespoons fresh mint leaves

Tips from Your Sponsor

Herbs contain essential oils that are extracted when steeped in hot water for a period of time. Covering the teapot with a lid prevents the oils from escaping with the steam. Mints have a strong fragrance and add flavor to teas that otherwise would be quite bland.

1. Pour boiling water over the flowers and mint leaves.

2. Cover and let steep for 10–15 minutes. Chill and serve.

CREAMY BASHED POTATOES

These mashed potatoes, though quite basic in nature, are far richer than any of the food Katniss has ever experienced. They're representative of the transition she's making when she's on her way from the Seam to the Capitol.
(*The Hunger Games*, Chapter 3)

Yields 4 servings

6 medium russet potatoes, peeled and cubed

½ cup warm milk or heavy cream

1 cup (2 sticks) butter

2 teaspoons kosher salt

Pepper to taste

Tips from Your Sponsor

Want a more adventurous twist on these mashed potatoes? Try mixing 3 cloves of crushed garlic in with the warm milk or cream before adding to the potatoes; then combine with a handful of grated Asiago cheese for a scrumptious yet unique garlic taste!

1. Place potatoes in a saucepan and cover completely with water. Cover and bring to boil.

2. Cook for 30–35 minutes or until very, very tender. Drain; return potatoes to saucepan.

3. Add milk, butter, salt, and pepper; mash with a potato masher until light and fluffy. For even creamier potatoes, add more milk.

SCALLOPED ONIONS AND APPLES CASSEROLE

Onions and apples are one of the few offerings that can be found throughout the forest outside the Seam. Onions can symbolize one's ability to peel through the layers and get to the heart of the situation at hand. With her father and Gale's help, Katniss is able to identify wild onions and pick a bounty of apples, thus making it possible for her to navigate both the woods and the Hunger Games, while perhaps digging through the layers of her own fears and needs.
(*The Hunger Games*, Chapter 4)

Yields 6–8 servings

3 sweet onions

5 apples

Kosher salt and freshly ground black pepper to taste

½ cup beef consommé

6 bacon strips

1 cup bread crumbs

Tips from Your Sponsor

For a quick baked onion dish, try the following: Slice 2–3 onions and place the layers in a casserole. Pour heavy cream over onions shy of completely covering, about 1–1½ cups. Sprinkle with Parmesan or Romano cheese and bake at 350°F for about 30–40 minutes, until bubbly and golden brown.

1. Preheat oven to 350°F. Grease a large baking dish and set aside.

2. Peel onions and slice thinly. Peel, core, and thinly slice the apples. Arrange alternating layers of onions and apples in the baking dish. Lightly season with salt and pepper to taste. (Remember that the consommé and bacon are salty.) Pour the consommé over all.

3. Fry the bacon until crisp. Remove to paper towels and let cool.

4. Drain all but 2 or 3 tablespoons of bacon grease from the skillet. Add the bread crumbs to the skillet and stir until brown. Crumble bacon over casserole, then sprinkle browned bread crumbs over the top.

5. Bake, covered, for 30 minutes. Uncover and bake an additional 10–15 minutes more. Serve hot or warm.

GOOSE LIVER PÂTÉ

Katniss smothers this rich goose liver pâté on buttermilk biscuits (see Katniss-Approved Puffy Buttermilk Biscuits, Chapter 2) while waiting for dinner in the Capitol, but, as is the case for many things within the Hunger Games universe, the pâté's meaning is more complicated than it may appear. After all, Katniss has quickly realized by now that she has to play by the rules if she's going to survive. If she doesn't her goose is cooked—just like her pâté.
(*The Hunger Games*, Chapter 6)

Yields 6–8 servings

1 pound goose livers

1 cup chicken broth

1 small onion, sliced

1 sprig fresh rosemary

8 cooked bacon strips, crumbled

½ cup (1 stick) unsalted butter, softened

2 tablespoons brandy or cognac

1 tablespoon Dijon mustard

Kosher salt and freshly cracked black pepper to taste

Tips from Your Sponsor

While Katniss prefers this pâté slathered on top of puffy bread, you can also serve the pâté in a porcelain or pottery crock with buttered toast points, rye crackers, or flatbread. This dish goes well with peperoncini, dates, and figs, as well.

1. Cut goose livers in half and simmer in chicken broth with onion and rosemary for about 15 minutes, until tender. Let cool. Reserve onion and ¼ cup of the broth. Remove leaves from the sprig of rosemary and chop fine.

2. In a food processor, combine livers, onion, reserved ¼ cup broth, chopped rosemary, crumbled bacon, butter, cognac, and mustard. Process until smooth. Season to taste with salt and pepper.

3. Spoon pâté into a covered container. Refrigerate overnight so flavors will blend. Will keep 3 or 4 days in the refrigerator.

GREEN WITH ENVY PESTO PASTA

Moments after consuming this delicious pesto pasta, Katniss looks up to see herself face-to-face with the young girl—now an Avox—that she and Gale were too scared to help. Pasta can represent becoming entangled or caught up in something, which is certainly what is happening to Katniss while she eats this delectable dish.
(*The Hunger Games*, Chapter 6)

Yields 4–6 servings

5 garlic cloves

¾ cup toasted walnuts

1 tablespoon granulated sugar

2½ cups grated fresh, high-quality Parmesan

2½ cups grated pecorino Romano

3 cups packed Italian basil leaves

2 cups packed basil leaves

1 tablespoon fresh ground pepper

½ cup extra-virgin olive oil

3 tablespoons fresh lemon juice

Pinch of lemon zest

1 pound whole wheat linguine

Tips from Your Sponsor

While most pesto recipes call for pine nuts, walnuts are far cheaper and much easier to find at your local supermarket. Also, the quality of pine nuts can vary depending on its region of origin; thus walnuts prove to be a safer, and more interesting, bet. Most gourmands won't even be able to taste the difference!

1. Pulse garlic in a food processor until finely chopped, then add walnuts, sugar, cheeses, a large handful of the herbs, and pepper. Process until completely chopped. Add remaining herbs and lemon juice and zest one handful at a time. Pulse after each addition, until finely chopped. With motor still running, add oil and blend until incorporated. For a silkier pesto, add more oil than directed.

2. Set aside 2/3 cup pesto in a large bowl. Cook linguine al dente, then add about ¼ cup pasta-cooking water into reserved pesto. Add drained pasta to pesto; toss well. Salt and pepper to taste. Serve with additional fresh Parmesan.

CAPITOL CREAMY SPINACH FETTUCCINE

Another pasta in green sauce provided by the Capitol, this is a creamier option than the previous Green with Envy Pesto Pasta. While both are delicious, this dish requires a hefty appetite. Don't plan on battling any mutant dogs after eating this filling meal!
(*The Hunger Games*, Chapter 6)

Yields 4–6 servings

½ pound dry fettuccine pasta

2 tablespoons unsalted butter

4 tablespoons cream cheese

1 cup whole milk

1 tablespoon all-purpose flour

1½ cups freshly grated Parmesan cheese

1 tablespoon extra-virgin olive oil

1 cup fresh spinach, chopped

¼ cup sun-dried tomatoes, chopped

½ cup fresh oregano, chopped

Tips from Your Sponsor

For some added protein, try adding grilled chicken or shrimp to this dish. On a diet? Feel free to nix the cream cheese, lessen the amount of Parmesan cheese, and use 1% condensed milk instead of whole milk. Whole wheat or rice pasta is another delicious option! These changes will still provide a thick and creamy fettuccine for you and your family.

1. Fill a large pot with lightly salted water. Bring water to boil. Add fettuccine, and cook for 15 minutes, or until pasta reaches desired consistency. Drain.

2. In a medium saucepan over medium heat, melt together butter and cream cheese. Once they reach a liquid composition, add whole milk and let simmer for three minutes. Whisk milk mixture, then mix in the flour to thicken. Stir in Parmesan cheese until melted then remove from heat.

3. In a separate saucepan, heat olive oil. Add spinach, sun-dried tomatoes, and oregano. Sauté for five minutes. Add mixture to butter sauce and cook for 3 minutes, stirring occasionally until heated through. Serve over cooked pasta.

RUE'S ROASTED ROOTS

Rue manages to collect a good mess of roots and nuts before she meets up with Katniss. These roots and nuts are indicative of Rue herself. Like her foraged goods, Rue is small and unassuming, but behind this exterior is someone strong and self-sufficient.
(*The Hunger Games*, Chapter 15)

Yields 8–10 servings

6 evening primrose roots, scraped and cut in small pieces

3 burdock roots, peeled and chopped

1 pound Jerusalem artichokes, scrubbed and sliced

½ cup coconut milk

¼ cup (½ stick) butter, melted

¼ cup maple syrup

2 tablespoons fresh gingerroot

2 tablespoons Wild Herb Seasoning (Chapter 3)

Tips from Your Sponsor

If you can't find burdock root, you can substitute carrots, a much more common root vegetable. Carrots, like many root vegetables, are a wonderful source of antioxidants, minerals, and that old standby, fiber. However, be careful! If you eat too many carrots your skin really can become orange thanks to a benign condition known as carotenosis. While such strangely colored skin would be in vogue at the Capitol, it might get you odd looks nowadays.

1. Preheat oven to 350°F.

2. Steam evening primrose roots and burdock roots 20 minutes, until tender.

3. In a 12" iron skillet, combine steamed roots with Jerusalem artichokes. Add the coconut milk, butter, maple syrup, and ginger. Coat vegetables with mixture.

4. Place the iron skillet into the oven. Roast about 20 minutes.

5. Remove from oven, toss and turn the roots, and then roast about 20 minutes more, until the roots are tender and nicely glazed. Sprinkle with Wild Herb Seasoning.

6. Serve as a side dish or over rice.

Humble Beginnings | 93

MIXED MESSAGES MIXED BERRY JAM

Though Peeta doesn't realize it, Katniss secretly mixes sleep syrup into a simpler version of this mixed berry jam so she can go to the dangerous feast and collect the medicine for his leg. That she mixes the sleep serum with berries foreshadows her and Peeta's deception with the poisonous berries at the end of the Hunger Games.
(*The Hunger Games*, Chapter 20)

Yields 4 half pints jam

1 pound blueberries

1 pound blackberries

2½ cups sugar

2 tablespoons fresh lemon juice

4 half-pint canning jars with lids and screw bands, thoroughly cleaned

Tips from Your Sponsor

If Steps 3 through 5 and 8 through 11 appear too difficult, don't let that deter you from trying this recipe! You don't have to can this jam. Sure, canning helps the jam last a great deal longer, but you can skip these steps and simply place your jam mixture into a clean jar. Store in the fridge for up to 2 weeks—more than enough time to thoroughly enjoy this treat!

1. In a large bowl, lightly crush all the berries between your fingers. Add sugar and lemon juice. Stir thoroughly. Let stand at room temperature for 2–2½ hours, stirring occasionally.

2. Place a saucer in the freezer.

3. Using a stockpot that is at least a couple of inches deeper than the height of your canning jars, place a metal rack at bottom to separate your jars from direct heat. Fill pot with water, cover, and heat water to a boil. Reduce heat to low. Keep simmering.

4. Place canning jar lids in a small saucepan. Cover lids with cold water and bring to a simmer. Turn off heat; leave lids in pan.

5. Fill canning jars with very, very hot water. Set aside.

6. Transfer fruit mixture to a large saucepan and bring to boil over medium-high heat, stirring occasionally. Using a potato masher, mash the mixture into a thick purée. Reduce heat to medium and boil gently until mixture begins to thicken, stirring often, about 20 minutes.

7. Remove saucepan from heat to test jam for jelling point. Drop 1 teaspoonful of jam on chilled saucer and place back in freezer for one minute. Remove saucer and push edge of jam with a fingertip. If jam has properly jelled, surface will gently wrinkle. If not, return saucepan to heat and cook jam for a few minutes longer. Repeat test.

8. Drain hot water from jars. Thoroughly shake out excess water. Ladle hot jam into each jar, leaving ½–¾ inch of space at top. Clean rim of each jar with a damp cloth. Using tongs, lift lids from the saucepan, remaining careful of their hot temperature. Shake lids dry and place atop jars. Seal each jar closed with a screw band, twisting to close (but not too tightly).

9. Place jam-filled jars back in hot water in stockpot. If necessary, add water to pot so jars are covered by at least 1 inch of water. Cover pot and bring to boil. Reduce heat and boil gently for another 7–10 minutes. Turn off heat and allow jars to remain in the water for 5 minutes.

10. Using tongs, remove jars from stockpot, being careful not to tilt them. Place upright on towel. Cool completely at room temperature, 3–5 hours. Jam will thicken as it cools.

HONEY, GOAT CHEESE, AND APPLE TART FROM THE MELLARK FAMILY BAKERY

As Peeta and Katniss prepare to fight the other last surviving tributes Cato and Foxface, the pair of heroes consume the last of the feast Haymitch and the sponsors sent them. While eating, Peeta mentions that his family makes a fancy tart of goat cheese and apples back at the bakery, and Katniss is astonished to learn that Peeta's family never gets to eat the fancy food they put on display, only the dry leftovers. This news helps Katniss realize she and Peeta have more in common than she previously believed. (*The Hunger Games*, Chapter 23)

Yields 16 tarts

16 frozen puff pastry shells, thawed

1 egg, beaten

5 ounces soft goat cheese

1½ teaspoons lemon juice

1 tablespoon sugar

1 cup honey

½ teaspoon kosher salt

4 medium Pink Lady or Cortland apples, peeled and cut into 1/8-inch-thick slices

3 tablespoons salted butter

½ teaspoon ground allspice

Tips from Your Sponsor

As you have likely realized, different apples have different tastes that can be utilized in your kitchen. The crispness of Pink Lady and Cortland apples works well with a tart, while the sweetness of a Fuji, McIntosh, or Jonagold apple would likely work better in a sauce.

1. Preheat oven to 350°F. Lightly oil two baking sheets.

2. Place 8 of the thawed puff pastry shells on each of the oiled baking sheets. Brush each shell with beaten egg.

3. Bake shells for 10 minutes.

4. While shells are baking, mix cheese, lemon juice, sugar, 1 tablespoon of the honey, and salt in bowl. Pour cheese mixture into a Ziploc bag. Cut the bottom edge of the bag, creating a makeshift piping bag, and squeeze mixture atop each prebaked pastry shell.

5. Artfully place apple slices atop cheese. Mix butter and ½ cup of the honey in a small bowl; brush over apples and tart. Sprinkle with allspice.

6. Bake tarts until apples are tender and pastry is lightly golden, about 15–20 minutes. While still warm, place tarts on plates. Drizzle some of remaining honey over each and serve warm.

FROM CASUAL TO FORMAL: FRUIT NUT SPREAD AT THE CAPITOL BANQUET

No banquet is complete without a fruit spread to smear on fancy breads and crackers! It's likely that this creamy, decadent spread would have been served at the Capitol banquet when Peeta and Katniss finished up their Victory Tour.
(*Catching Fire*, Chapter 6)

Yields 8–10 servings

1 cup wild berries, mashed

¾ cup nuts, finely chopped

8 ounces cream cheese, softened

¼ cup maple yogurt

Tips from Your Sponsor

This recipe allows for some creativity. It's up to you and your personal tastes as to what kind of nuts and berries to use. Almonds are always a delicious option, as are blueberries and strawberries. Try serving on herbed crostini for a crunchier (not to mention saltier) bite.

1. Stir wild berries and nuts into cream cheese and yogurt until creamy and smooth.

2. Use as a spread on bread or crackers.

OFF-YOUR-CHEST ROASTED CHESTNUTS

It's while roasting chestnuts in the abandoned house on the lake that Katniss comes clean to Gale. The roasting chestnuts represent the slow-burning fire of rebellion that Katniss ignited in the arena. (*Catching Fire*, Chapter 7)

Yields 6 servings

2 dozen chestnuts

Tips from Your Sponsor

Try roasting these chestnuts over an open fire to capture the wood flavor of the smoke!

1. Preheat oven to 400°F.

2. Cut an X into each chestnut on the flat side.

3. Place on a baking sheet and bake for 30–35 minutes, turning frequently.

4. Remove from oven and let cool for ten minutes. Peel while still warm.

BUTTERY PARSLEY MASHED POTATOES

As only the best comfort food can, the warmth of these parsley mashed potatoes helps lighten Katniss's down spirits before the opening ceremony. The potatoes and herbs likely make Katniss think briefly of home before Cinna dresses her for the evening.
(*Catching Fire*, Chapter 15)

Yields 4–6 servings

2 pounds Yukon Gold potatoes, cleaned and peeled

¾ cup ricotta cheese

½ cup (1 stick) butter, softened

½–1 cup whole milk

½ cup fresh parsley, chopped

Kosher salt to taste

Fresh ground pepper to taste

Tips from Your Sponsor

Parsley is an herb that is incredibly useful in the wild. Not only does parsley tea help control blood pressure, but when crushed and rubbed on your skin, it may lessen the itching of mosquito bites!

1. Place potatoes in a large pot of salted water. Bring water to boil over high heat. Reduce heat to medium high. Cover and cook until potatoes are tender, about 45–60 minutes.

2. Drain potatoes and return them to the pot. Roughly mash with a potato masher.

3. Add ricotta cheese, butter, ½ cup milk, and parsley. Mash potatoes until smooth, adding more milk if necessary. Season to taste with salt and pepper.

JEWEL-COLORED MINT JELLY

The jewel-colored jelly that accompanies the Roast Pheasant (Chapter 6) served at the lunch before the opening ceremonies can only reinforce for the tributes the wealth and power of the Capitol. (*Catching Fire*, Chapter 15)

Yields 4 ½-pint jars

1½ cups fresh mint leaves and stems

2¼ cups pineapple juice

3 tablespoons lemon juice

3 drops green food coloring

3½ cups white sugar

3 ounces liquid pectin

Tips from Your Sponsor

Making jelly is no easy task. Don't give up hope if your first attempt doesn't set . . . just try again. For a more tart jelly, reduce the sugar to just 2 cups, or use water instead of pineapple juice.

1. Rinse off the mint leaves, and place them into a large saucepan. Crush with a potato masher. Add pineapple juice, and bring mixture to a boil. Remove from heat, cover, and let stand for 10 minutes. Strain, measuring out 1⅔ cups of the liquid. Discard remaining liquid.

2. Pour the reserved juice into a saucepan. Stir in the lemon juice and food coloring. Mix in the sugar, and place the pan over high heat, stirring constantly. Bring to a boil. While stirring, add pectin. Continue to stir constantly while allowing mixture to boil for a full minute.

3. Transfer mixture to hot sterile jars and seal.

4. Place a rack at the bottom of a large stockpot and fill halfway with water. Bring to a boil over high heat, then carefully lower the jars into the pot. Leave a 2" space between jars. Pour in more boiling water if necessary until the water is at least 1 inch above the tops of the jars. Bring to a full boil, cover the pot, and let sit for fifteen minutes. Remove and cool in fridge.

QUARTER QUELL NUTTY GRANOLA

During the Quarter Quell, Katniss tosses out nuts such as the ones used in this recipe to determine the location of the powerful force field. The fact that Katniss uses nuts to solve the force field's riddle is purposeful. After all, the location of the force field is a tough nut to crack! (*Catching Fire*, Chapter 20)

Yields 6–8 servings

10 cups rolled oats

1 cup wheat germ

½ cup ground flaxseed

1½ cups oat bran

1½ cups almonds, finely chopped

1½ cups walnuts, finely chopped

1½ cups cashews, finely chopped

1½ teaspoons salt

½ cup maple syrup

½ cup brown sugar

½ cup honey

1 cup vegetable oil

2 tablespoons ground cinnamon

1 tablespoon vanilla extract

2 cups raisins

Tips from Your Sponsor

For a sweeter granola, try adding a cup of chocolate chips or M&M's instead of raisins. A cup of shredded coconut added before baking also brings a unique flavor.

1. Preheat oven to 325°F. Line two large baking sheets with parchment paper.

2. Combine the oats, wheat germ, ground flaxseed, oat bran, almonds, walnuts, and cashews in a large bowl.

3. Stir together salt, maple syrup, brown sugar, honey, oil, cinnamon, and vanilla in a saucepan. Bring to a boil over medium heat, and then pour over the dry ingredients, stirring to coat. Spread out the mixture evenly on the baking sheets.

4. Bake in the preheated oven until crispy and toasted, about 20 minutes. Stir once halfway through.

5. Cool granola and allow to slightly harden, and then stir in the raisins. Store cooled granola in an airtight container.

PROPOS GRILLED CHEESE SANDWICH

After agreeing to be the face of the rebellion, Katniss, Gale, and various members of their team explore the outskirts of Katniss's old home — specifically the Meadow. Before launching into a heartbreaking song sung to her by her father, Katniss and the troops enjoy a cheese sandwich — a meal that, like Katniss's memories, harkens back to childhood.
(*Mockingjay*, Chapter 9)

Yields 2 sandwiches

4 slices sourdough bread
4 tablespoons (½ stick) butter, softened
4 slices sharp Cheddar cheese

Tips from Your Sponsor

For a healthier version of this recipe, use mayonnaise in lieu of the butter. It's more spreadable, and has a lower calorie count! Also, try lettuce or thinly sliced apples along with the cheese in this classic sandwich for an extra nutritious bite.

1. Preheat skillet on low to medium heat. Generously butter one side of slice of bread. Place bread buttered side down in skillet and top with two slices of cheese. Butter a second slice of bread on one side and place buttered side up on top of cheese.

2. Grill until bottom slice is lightly browned. Flip sandwich over and continue grilling until cheese is melted. Repeat with remaining ingredients.

FRESH CORN PUDDING FOR PEETA

After he's been emotionally hijacked, it's big news when Peeta is allowed to feed himself pudding, a soft, gentle food made for those who are having difficulty eating or who just need to taste something soothing. This pudding, while not sweet, works as a filling meal for when we need a little comfort in their own lives.
(*Mockingjay*, Chapter 14)

Yields 6–8 servings

2 cups fresh corn kernels (about 5 large ears)

1 fire-roasted red pepper, chopped

6 green onions, chopped

2 tablespoons flour

2 teaspoons sugar

1 teaspoon kosher salt

¼ teaspoon red pepper flakes

3 eggs

1½ cups heavy cream

Tips from Your Sponsor

Lacking red pepper flakes? A ¼ teaspoon of cayenne pepper or hot paprika will work in a pinch. This dish is best when made with fresh corn from the farmer's market.

1. Preheat oven to 350°F. Grease a 1½-quart casserole and set aside.

2. Combine corn, pepper, and onions in a large bowl.

3. Blend flour, sugar, salt, and red pepper flakes together and add to corn mixture.

4. Beat eggs and cream together and add to corn mixture, stirring well. Pour into the greased casserole. Place dish in a larger shallow pan filled with 1 inch of water. Bake in the oven for about 1 hour, or until a knife inserted in the middle comes out clean.

LIVER PÂTÉ

Liver represents suffering and torture (remember Prometheus?). That's exactly how Tigris feels when she serves liver pâté to Katniss and overhears Peeta and Gale talking about whom Katniss will chose to be with after the war.
(*Mockingjay*, Chapter 24)

Yields 4 servings

1 pound Braunschweiger liver sausage, cooked and cut into pieces

1 tablespoon whole milk

2 tablespoons butter, softened

1 tablespoon plus 1 teaspoon finely chopped onion

1 (8-ounce) package cream cheese, softened

1½ teaspoons sugar

½ teaspoon minced garlic

1½ teaspoons chili powder

1 tablespoon Worcestershire sauce

1 teaspoon parsley

1 teaspoon dill

Tips from Your Sponsor

While the most famous pâté is foie gras, made from the fatty livers of geese, this is a simple substitute that will be a hit at any party. Try with mini sourdough bread crackers or herbed crackers, easily found at your local market.

1. Line a loaf pan with waxed paper. In a medium bowl, stir together the sausage, milk, butter, onion, and cream cheese. Add sugar, garlic, chili powder, and Worcestershire sauce. Mix until well blended. Pour into prepared loaf pan. Sprinkle parsley and dill over the top of the pâté.

2. Cover loaf pan and chill in refrigerator for at least 2 hours. Remove from pan and discard waxed paper. Serve pâté with crackers.

CHAPTER 5

SINK OR SWIM–SEAFOOD

Throughout The Hunger Games trilogy our heroes are saved and sustained by their knowledge of and their connection to nature. This knowledge allows them to feed themselves, an act representing their self-sufficiency—a trait not found in those in the Capitol, who must rely on others. Two of the most self-sufficient men in The Hunger Games trilogy, Finnick Odair of District 4—the fishing district—and Gale, Katniss's friend from District 12, count fishing among their skills. In this chapter, you'll find delicious seafood recipes that may make you long to wield a trident or cast a line as well.

SMOKED WHITEFISH WITH HORSERADISH SAUCE

Fishing was a means for Katniss and Gale to not only survive, but a way for them to unwind from their stressful lives as well. It's likely that they used a spicy recipe like this one a great deal on those dreary, never-ending days of desolation.
(*The Hunger Games*, Chapter 8)

Yields 4 servings

2 pounds whitefish fillets (4 fillets)

½ cup heavy cream

2–3 tablespoons prepared horseradish

4 cups salad greens

1 lemon, quartered

Tips from Your Sponsor

Like Katniss, whitefish are survivors. They've been around since the end of the last glaciation, about 12,000 years ago! Since then, they've diversified into different populations, with two different ecotypes recognized within the species—a normal one and a dwarf. The type of whitefish that Katniss is most likely to pursue is lake whitefish, or *Coregonus clupeaformis*, which is found throughout North America in areas such as Minnesota, Michigan, and throughout the Great Lakes region.

1. Prepare a small-to-medium sized fire in a smoker or grill. Place 3 water-soaked wood chunks, untreated maple or cherry, on the fire.

2. Place the whitefish in the smoker or on the indirect-heat side of the grill. Close the lid.

3. Smoke for 1–1½ hours. When done, whitefish should flake easily when pierced with a fork.

4. Whip the heavy cream in a bowl. Stir in the horseradish to taste. Refrigerate until ready to use.

5. To serve, place 1 cup of the greens on each serving plate. Top each with a fish fillet. Spoon a little of the horseradish sauce over each fillet and garnish with a lemon quarter. Serve remaining sauce in a dish on the side.

FIRE-ROASTED TROUT WITH SLIVERED VEGETABLES

Unfortunately, Katniss doesn't have time to make this delicious trout, as she has to spend all her time in the arena trying to stay alive. When you're in the mood to cook over a fire rather than running from one, try this meal, in which we replace lily roots with more festive bell peppers.
(*The Hunger Games*, Chapter 12)

Yields 4 servings

2 tablespoons vegetable oil

4 (12-ounce) whole trout, cleaned

2 lemons, sliced

1 red bell pepper, seeded and slivered

1 yellow bell pepper, seeded and slivered

1 red onion, peeled and slivered

8 ounces mushrooms, sliced

1 teaspoon fresh rosemary leaves, chopped

½ cup white wine vinegar

2 tablespoons Dijon mustard

Salt and pepper to taste

Tips from Your Sponsor

Cooking food in aluminum foil makes for very easy cleanup. This is a great way to cook on the grill, in the embers of a fire as Katniss did, or in the oven. You can also buy ready-made foil packets that are extra heavy duty for larger fish and game.

1. Prepare a hot fire in your grill or preheat the oven to 375°F.

2. Lightly oil four pieces of aluminum foil and place 1 trout on each. Place several slices of lemon in the cavity of each fish. Distribute the peppers, onions, and mushrooms evenly over the trout. Sprinkle ¼ teaspoon of the rosemary across the top of each.

3. Whisk together the white wine vinegar and mustard. Drizzle about 2½ tablespoons of the mixture over each trout. Season with salt and pepper to taste.

4. Tightly wrap the foil around the fish. Grill or bake the foil packets for about 20–25 minutes.

5. Place a packet on each of four dinner plates. Diners should be cautioned to open their packets carefully, as there will be a burst of hot steam.

CRAB CAKES FOR CRABBY SPIRITS (WITH CILANTRO-LIME DIPPING SAUCE)

Before posing for her wedding photos, Katniss learns that crab is unavailable in the Capitol. This catches her by surprise, which is typical of the sideways walking crab that takes things in a totally different direction than expected. If crabmeat were plentiful, you can be sure those in the Capitol would be eating these crab cakes.
(*Catching Fire*, Chapter 12)

Yields 4–6 servings

> Crab Cakes:

1 pound crabmeat, dried well

1 cup Ritz crackers, crushed

3 green onions, finely chopped

1 bell pepper, finely chopped

¼ cup celery, finely chopped

¼ cup mayonnaise

1 egg

1 teaspoon Worcestershire sauce

1 teaspoon honey mustard

1 lemon, juiced

½ teaspoon garlic powder

1 teaspoon sea salt

Dash of cayenne pepper

Flour for dusting

1 cup (2 sticks) butter

> Dipping Sauce:

1/3 cup nonfat Greek yogurt

2 tablespoons mayonnaise

2 tablespoons fresh cilantro, minced

¼ teaspoon jalapeño, minced

Zest and juice of 1 large lime

1. In a large bowl, mix together all ingredients for the crab cakes except the flour and butter. Shape mixture into patties and dust with flour. Chill patties in fridge for one hour.

2. In a small bowl, combine all ingredients for the dipping sauce. Mix well and set aside.

3. Heat butter in a large skillet over medium heat. When hot, carefully place 2 crab cakes in pan and fry until browned, about 5 minutes. Carefully flip and fry the other side, about 4 minutes. Remove and keep warm. Repeat until all crab cakes are cooked.

4. Serve crab cakes warm with dipping sauce.

Tips from Your Sponsor

For a slightly healthier option, try baking your crab cakes instead of frying them. Simply prepare as listed, but instead of placing in a large skillet, place crab patties in a large baking dish. Cover patties with 1½ cups melted butter and bake at 375°F for 20 minutes (flipping them after 10 minutes), or until golden brown.

KATNISS'S BAKED SHAD FOR PEETA

While Peeta and Katniss battle not only the blood-thirsty tributes but their hunger as well, Katniss catches a few small, bony fish, or shad, and makes a meal out of them. The bones in the shad mirror the skin and bones that our heroes are slowly becoming.
(*The Hunger Games*, Chapter 21)

Yields 4 servings

1 (3–4 pound) whole shad, cleaned

2 tablespoons extra-virgin olive oil

½ teaspoon garlic salt

1 teaspoon lemon pepper

½ cup toasted pine nuts, divided

4 green onions

1 lemon, halved

½ cup white grape juice

Tips from Your Sponsor

This slow method of cooking the shad helps to soften the many bones inside the meat, making them almost edible. However, if you'd prefer to smoke your fish, you can place the foil-encased shad on a smoker at 225°F. Cook for one hour with foil open so that the wood smoke can penetrate. Tightly close the foil and then cook for an additional 4–5 hours.

1. Preheat the oven to 250°F. Lightly grease a deep disposable aluminum pan large enough to hold the shad.

2. Lightly coat shad with the olive oil. Sprinkle inside and out with the garlic salt and lemon pepper. Place 2 tablespoons of the pine nuts and all the green onions in the cavity of the fish. Set fish in pan and sprinkle remaining pine nuts on top of it. Squeeze the juice of both lemon halves over the fish.

3. Pour the grape juice into the pan. Cover tightly with heavy-duty foil.

4. Bake in oven for 5 hours. Serve with sauce spooned over each serving. For extra flavor, serve with wild rice.

SHAD ROE

Katniss could certainly try this option for cooking shad on those treacherous nights when she can't risk a fire. However, finding shad roe in the amount Katniss would need to make this dish isn't very likely. (*The Hunger Games,* Chapter 21)

Yields 4 small servings

2 tablespoons unsalted butter

3 tablespoons onion, minced

2 pair shad roe (about 1½ pounds)

1 cup white grape juice

1 bay leaf, broken in half

1 tablespoon fresh lemon juice

Kosher salt and pepper to taste

1 teaspoon cornstarch

1 cup heavy cream

2 tablespoons onion chives, snipped

Tips from Your Sponsor

Roe is considered a delicacy in countries such as China and India. To impress your friends, try serving this along with a few other fancy seafood appetizers for an appetizer-only dinner party. Not only will this stop people from stuffing themselves until they are sick, but it will allow for a variety of food choices that many of your guests might not ever have had the opportunity to try.

1. Melt the butter in a large skillet over medium heat. Add the onion and cook for 1 minute. Add the shad roe and sauté for 1 minute on each side. Add the grape juice, bay leaf, lemon juice, and salt and pepper to taste. Gently simmer, uncovered, until the roe is just barely firm, about 10 minutes.

2. Remove the roe with a slotted spoon, leaving the poaching liquid in the skillet. Cool the roe and then trim off the tough membrane on either side. Slice the roe and set aside.

3. Cook poaching liquid over high heat until reduced by half. Remove the bay leaf.

4. Add the cornstarch to 2 tablespoons of the heavy cream and stir to blend. Add the mixture to poaching liquid with the rest of the cream and stir until thickened. Add chives.

5. Pour cream sauce into a pretty, shallow serving bowl and place roe in the sauce. Give everyone a plate, fork, spoon, and slices of crusty bread, and let them serve themselves.

FINNICK'S OLD-FASHIONED CLAMBAKE

When Finnick manages to catch a large amount of shellfish, he feeds them to his allies in the arena, which is appropriate considering the social aspect of a clambake. Its with this meal that we witness the tributes starting to bond together as friends—or at least allies.
(*Catching Fire*, Chapter 22)

Yields 8 servings

8 ears of corn, unshucked

8 pounds steamer clams, rinsed under running water

1 pound unsalted butter, melted

1 teaspoon liquid smoke flavoring

2 teaspoons barbecue seasoning

2 pounds new potatoes, parboiled, threaded onto metal skewers.

Tips from Your Sponsor

The New England clambake is a traditional method of cooking foods, usually on a beach. You can supplement the seafood (commonly steamers, crabs, lobster, and mussels) with potatoes, sausages, carrots, and onions. Try a variation of ingredients to develop your own traditional clambake.

1. Turn on the grill. When hot, grill the corn directly over the flames for 4 minutes per side, 8 minutes total. Turn only once, halfway through grilling. Remove and keep warm.

2. Place the clams on the grill rack, discarding any that have already opened. Close the lid and grill until the clams have opened, about 10 minutes. Discard any clams that have not opened. Remove and keep warm.

3. In bowl, stir together the melted butter, smoke flavoring, and barbecue seasoning. Brush the potato skewers with the mixture, reserving the remaining butter mixture. Arrange the skewers on the grill rack, close the lid, and grill for 5 minutes per side or until done.

4. To serve, shuck the corn and then place the corn, clams, and potato skewers on a platter. Drizzle the corn and clams with remaining butter mixture and serve.

SPICY SEAFOOD GUMBO

Another popular recipe from District 4, gumbo dates all the way back to seventeenth-century Louisiana. The spicy red sauce here is similar to the spicy sauce that the tributes eat right before all hell breaks loose when Katniss breaks the force field. The fiery flavoring foreshadows this event by telling us that, like the shrimp, the events in the arena are going to become even hotter than they've been before. (*Catching Fire*, Chapter 25)

Yields 4–6 servings

½ cup (1 stick) butter

¼ cup all-purpose flour

1 medium white onion, chopped

2 cloves garlic, minced

2 stalks celery, diced

4 green onions, sliced

1 small green bell pepper, diced

2 fresh tomatoes, chopped

1 cup okra, sliced

1 cup clam juice or fish stock

2 tablespoons seafood seasoning

2 tablespoons Louisiana-style hot sauce

½ teaspoon ground cayenne pepper

2 pounds medium shrimp, peeled and deveined

Tips from Your Sponsor

There are two types of gumbo: Cajun and Creole. Cajun is usually identified by its dark roux (which is made often with okra or filé powder), while Creole gumbo is less spicy and often uses seafood with tomatoes and a thickener.

1. Heat butter in a heavy skillet over medium heat. Gradually stir in flour. Pressing the flat side of a large fork to the bottom of the pan in a side-to-side motion, stir constantly until the mixture turns dark, at least 15 minutes. It is very important to stir constantly. Do not let it burn! This cooked mixture, called roux, is your base sauce.

2. Once the roux is browned, add the onions, garlic, celery, green onions, and bell pepper to the skillet. Sauté for about 5 minutes to soften vegetables.

3. Stir in the chopped tomatoes, okra, and clam juice or fish stock, and add the seafood seasoning. Reduce heat to low, and simmer for about 20 minutes, stirring occasionally.

4. Season the sauce with hot pepper sauce and cayenne pepper. Add shrimp. Cook for about 15 minutes, or until the shrimp are opaque.

CHAPTER 6

DON'T CALL ME CHICKEN—POULTRY DISHES FOR THE BRAVE

Katniss's fans and enemies alike can attest that she is no chicken, though a great many of the dishes Katniss enjoys inside and outside of the Capitol are poultry-based. In this chapter, you'll find recipes such as Moist Chicken in Basil Cream Sauce, Grilled Blue Cheese Stuffed Groosling Breast, and Fall-off-the-Bone Tender Duck, all of which will remind you to stand your ground, be brave, and never let anyone call you chicken.

BRINED AND BAGGED WILD TURKEY

Katniss isn't the only one who profited from her hunting ability. Her skills helped feed not only her own and Gale's family, but the baker, the butcher, and other members of the Seam. The fact that one turkey feeds so many people reminds us of the community feelings present at Thanksgiving, when the turkey is the main event.
(*The Hunger Games*, Chapter 4)

Yields 6–8 servings

Lemon Brine (see below)

1 (10–12 pound) whole wild turkey

Corn Bread and Italian Sausage Stuffing (see following)

1 large stuffing bag

4 tablespoons olive oil

1 large oven-roasting bag

> Lemon Brine:

4 quarts water

1 cup kosher salt

1 cup dark brown sugar

½ cup lemon juice

Yields 8–10 servings

> Corn Bread and Italian Sausage Stuffing:

½ cup (1 stick) butter

1 cup celery, chopped

1 medium onion, chopped

1 jalapeño pepper, seeded and chopped

3 cups chicken broth

4 cups corn bread, crumbled

4 slices sourdough bread, toasted and cubed

½ pound Italian sausage, spicy or mild, casings removed

Giblets from turkey, chopped (optional)

1 teaspoon dried sage (or substitute rosemary)

Kosher salt and freshly ground pepper to taste

2 eggs, beaten

1. Combine brine ingredients in a large container, preferably one with a handle for pouring.

2. Place 2 or 3 buckets of ice in the bottom of a large cooler. Place turkey in a large plastic bag (such as a garbage bag) and set on top of the ice. Pour the brine into the bag and close with a twist tie. Add more ice as needed to keep cool, and brine for 8–12 hours. When the brining is nearly complete, make the stuffing.

> For the Corn Bread and Italian Sausage Stuffing:

3. Melt the butter in a large skillet and sauté the celery, onion, and pepper for 5 minutes or until soft. Add the chicken broth and heat until warm.

4. Place the crumbled corn bread and toasted bread cubes in a large bowl. Add the vegetable and chicken broth mixture and mix well.

5. In the skillet, brown the Italian sausage. Add the chopped giblets and cook until done, about 5–7 minutes. Add the sage or rosemary and stir to blend.

6. Add the sausage and giblets to the bread mixture and mix well. Taste and then season with salt and pepper. Add the eggs and mix well again.

7. Place the stuffing loosely in a large stuffing bag. Any stuffing that doesn't fit can be transferred to a buttered casserole dish and refrigerated, to be baked in the oven with the turkey.

8. Preheat oven to 350°F.

9. Remove turkey from the brine; rinse thoroughly with cold water and pat dry. Lightly coat turkey with the 4 tablespoons olive oil. Place the stuffing bag in the cavity of the turkey.

10. Prepare the large roasting bag according to the manufacturer's instructions. Place the stuffed turkey in the floured bag. Place bagged turkey in a roasting pan and secure the tie. Cut six ½" slits in the top of the bag.

11. Place the pan in the oven and roast turkey for 2½ hours. If you have extra stuffing to bake in a casserole dish, put it in the oven, uncovered, along with the turkey about 45–50 minutes before the turkey will be done.

12. Remove turkey from oven. If you had extra stuffing, remove the casserole dish and keep the stuffing warm until serving.

13. Carefully slit open the roasting bag, and then, using tongs, carefully pull the stuffing bag out of the turkey. Let turkey rest for 15–20 minutes before carving.

Tips from Your Sponsor

While brining your turkey might seem like extra effort, it's actually the easiest way to guarantee yourself a moist and flavorful turkey. It is important that your turkey *not* be a self-brining or kosher one, as those tend to be too salty due to their added stock. Instead, use a fresh natural or thawed turkey for best results.

MR. EVERDEEN'S GOOSE CONFIT

Katniss would often go hunting with her father when he went searching for waterfowl to feed the family. It's likely that the father/daughter pair would hunt for goose, a bird with an excellent navigation system. Just like the goose Mr. Everdeen would likely catch, Katniss, thanks to her father's love, knows how to find her way.
(*The Hunger Games*, Chapter 3)

Yields 4–6 servings

1 goose, preferably fatty
1 cup coarse kosher salt
4 cloves garlic, halved
8 whole cloves
12 whole peppercorns
2 cups peanut oil, if needed

Tips from Your Sponsor

Confit is a way to preserve goose or duck by salting, slow cooking, and immersing in fat. The word comes from the French verb *confire*, which means to preserve.

1. Cut the goose into 6 pieces. Sprinkle all over with the salt and place in a large baking dish. Cover the dish with plastic wrap and refrigerate for 24 hours, turning the goose pieces several times.

2. Remove the goose from the refrigerator and wipe off all the salt and juice with paper towels. Cut the visible fat off the goose and place the fat in a large pot with the garlic, cloves, and peppercorns. Add 2 tablespoons water and heat until the goose fat is almost melted.

3. Place goose pieces in the pot and add peanut oil to barely cover the meat, if needed. Cover and cook over medium heat for about 1 hour or until

juice runs clear from a leg joint when pierced with a knife and the meat is fork tender. Remove meat from pot, cool, and debone.

4. Place the meat in a glass or earthenware container and cover completely with the strained fat and cooking oil. Store in the refrigerator for 1 week to bring the flavor to its height. It will keep for at least 1 month refrigerated and may also be frozen for up to a year.

5. When ready to serve, simply wipe the goose meat clean of any excess fat. The meat can be served as is or browned in a skillet and warmed through.

ORANGE YOU GLAD I'M CHICKEN

After an exhausting day being "remade" in the Remake Center, Katniss isn't in the mood to enjoy yet another feast while her family starves back in District 12. Luckily, her stylist, Cinna, encourages her to eat her fill of this delectable orange dish—fitting because, traditionally, oranges represent prosperity, which Katniss hopes to win in the arena.
(*The Hunger Games*, Chapter 5)

Yields 4 servings

2 cups orange juice

5 tablespoons orange extract

1 tablespoon honey

½ cup olive oil

1 teaspoon salt

1 onion, chopped

2 cloves garlic, chopped

4 skinless, boneless chicken breast halves, pounded to ½" thickness

½ cup heavy cream

3 tablespoons cornstarch

4 tablespoons olive oil

½ cup flour

1 cup canned mandarin orange segments, drained

Tips from Your Sponsor

Not a huge fan of cream sauce? You can substitute the marinade (otherwise discarded once you start grilling the chicken) as your sauce for this dish. To kill any germs, cook marinade thoroughly once added to the chicken in the skillet.

1. Combine the orange juice, 2 tablespoons of the orange extract, honey, oil, salt, onions, and garlic in a bowl. Mix well.

2. Pierce chicken breasts with a fork several times so marinade can penetrate the meat. Place each breast half in its own large Ziploc bag. Pour orange juice marinade over each half to evenly coat. You will use all of your marinade.

3. Place bags in a large bowl to catch any drips. Place bowl in fridge. Let chicken marinate for at least 4 hours.

4. Combine heavy cream, cornstarch, and remaining 3 tablespoons orange extract in a small bowl.

5. Heat the 4 tablespoons olive oil in skillet over medium heat. Remove chicken from bags and lightly coat with flour. Place chicken in hot skillet and brown on both sides.

6. Stir in heavy cream mixture and orange segments. Simmer cream mixture until liquid has reduced by half. Remove chicken from pan when no longer pink in center, and allow sauce to reduce for another 3 minutes. Serve over rice.

MOIST CHICKEN IN BASIL CREAM SAUCE

If orange chicken isn't your thing, this alternatively creamy concoction should please the pickiest of eaters at the Capitol. It's while indulging in such delicious chicken delicacies that Katniss realizes her family could never afford even a skimpy chicken; they'd have to make do with wild turkey. Again, this juxtaposes the difference between the haves and the have-nots and reminds us of the wild influences her lifestyle has had on Katniss.
(*The Hunger Games*, Chapter 5)

Yields 4 servings

¼ cup whole milk

½ cup dried bread crumbs

4 tablespoons (½ stick) butter

3 garlic cloves, chopped

¼ cup chopped scallions

4 skinless, boneless chicken breasts

½ cup white wine

1 cup heavy whipping cream

½ cup grated fresh Parmesan cheese

¼ cup chopped fresh basil

¼ teaspoon ground black pepper

Tips from Your Sponsor

Basil is one of the many herbs Katniss and her father would be able to easily identify. Katniss would especially find basil helpful during the Hunger Games, as basil is extremely toxic to mosquitoes and other insects.

1. Place milk and bread crumbs in separate small bowls. In skillet, heat butter on medium heat. Add 2 of the chopped garlic cloves and the scallions to skillet. Sauté for 1 minute.

2. Dip chicken in the milk, then coat evenly with the bread crumbs. Cook chicken in the butter until juices run clear, about 10 minutes per side. Remove from pan and keep warm.

3. Add wine to skillet. Bring to boil over medium heat. Stir in cream; boil and stir for about a minute. Reduce heat.

4. Add Parmesan cheese, basil, pepper, and the last clove of garlic. Stir sauce and cook until heated through. Pour mixture over chicken and serve.

RUE AND KATNISS'S
APPLE-SMOKED GROOSLING

Katniss describes groosling as appearing similar to a small wild turkey. Thus, while we have no such animal, we can cook turkey in a way similar to Rue and Katniss's after they form their alliance. This turkey, well smoked over a fire, won't be quite as fatty as the groosling, but it will be just as delicious. (*The Hunger Games*, Chapter 15)

Yields 2 servings

½ cup balsamic vinegar

2 tablespoons water

1 tablespoon paprika

1 tablespoon kosher salt

1 tablespoon lemon pepper

¼ teaspoon marjoram

2 (1½–2 pound) wild turkey breast halves

Tips from Your Sponsor

Smoking is a form of slow cooking, with wood as the key flavor. The fire should be low, between 225°F and 300°F. Whole birds, whole fish, large roasts, ribs, and tough meats do well smoked slowly. Slow-smoked food is cooked until it's well done.

1. Combine the vinegar, water, paprika, salt, lemon pepper, and marjoram in a glass jar and shake to blend.

2. Place the turkey breasts in a large Ziploc bag. Pour the marinade over the turkey and carefully seal the bag, removing most of the air. Refrigerate for about 1–2 hours.

3. Build an indirect fire in a kettle grill or water smoker and add 3 or 4 water-soaked apple-wood chunks to the fire.

4. Remove the turkey breasts from the marinade and place on the indirect-heat side of the grill or smoker (discard remaining marinade). Slow smoke at 225°F for about 1½–2 hours or until a thermometer inserted into the thickest portion of the breast meat registers 165°F–170°F for well done. The turkey will retain a slightly pink color from the slow smoking and the wood.

5. Slice and serve.

GRILLED BLUE CHEESE STUFFED GROOSLING BREAST

Even if turkey breast isn't quite as moist as groosling, the blue cheese and olive oil in this recipe will provide a succulent sample of the kind of juicy meat groosling provides—sans the groosling and the horrible fighting for your life, of course.
(*The Hunger Games*, Chapter 15)

Yields 4–6 servings

2 (2-pound) turkey breast halves

½ cup crumbled high-quality blue cheese, plus more for garnish

2 tablespoons golden raisins, plus more for garnish

2 tablespoons Italian parsley, chopped, plus more for garnish

2 tablespoons extra-virgin olive oil

2 tablespoons Dijon mustard

2 tablespoons lemon juice

Tips from Your Sponsor

Don't forget that the temperature of meat cooked in the oven, on the grill, or in a sauté pan continues to rise another 5-plus degrees Fahrenheit after the meat is removed from its heat source. So if overcooking has been a problem, take meat off the heat a bit sooner, or 5 degrees short of the temperature desired for doneness.

1. Slice a pocket in each turkey breast and stuff with blue cheese, raisins, and parsley. Set meat in a shallow, well-oiled dish.

2. In a small bowl, whisk together the olive oil, Dijon mustard, and lemon juice. Pour over the turkey breasts. Cover with plastic wrap and marinate in the refrigerator for about 2–4 hours, turning two or three times.

3. When ready to grill, prepare a hot fire.

4. Remove turkey from marinade (discard remaining marinade). Sear the meat over the hot fire for about 5 minutes on each side. Move turkey to indirect-heat side of the grill and cover with the lid. Continue to cook for another 20 minutes or until the turkey breast meat registers 170°F on a meat thermometer when inserted in the thickest part of the breast meat for well-done. Be sure to make sure the thermometer reads the temperature of the meat and not the cheese.

5. Let turkey rest for about 5 minutes. Then slice on the diagonal. Present on a platter with garnish of parsley, crumbled blue cheese, and golden raisins.

KATNISS'S PICNIC CHICKEN SALAD

Even though there's no need for Katniss to hunt after she wins the Hunger Games, she still chooses to do so; hunting represents freedom for Katniss, something in short demand for her after the games. This chicken salad is easy enough to take along on a quick hunt.
(*Catching Fire*, Chapter 2)

Yields 6–8 servings

4 cooked boneless, skinless chicken breast halves, shredded

3 stalks celery, diced

5 green onions, chopped

1 Granny Smith apple, diced

¼ teaspoon ground black pepper

½ teaspoon curry powder

½ teaspoon sea salt

¾ to 1 cup mayonnaise

Tips from Your Sponsor

If you're not a fan of curry, try substituting 1 tablespoon dried parsley flakes, 2 teaspoons lemon juice, ½ teaspoon ground ginger, and a dash of Worcestershire sauce! Be sure to add salt and pepper to taste.

1. In a large bowl, mix together the chicken, celery, onions, apple, pepper, curry powder, salt, and enough mayonnaise to suit your personal preference. Mix until evenly coated.

2. Chill for at least 3 hours (preferably overnight for curry flavors to fully infiltrate the salad).

PRESIDENT SNOW'S SAUTÉED DOVE BREASTS IN BACON DRIPPINGS

It comes as no surprise that someone as evil as President Snow would enjoy a meal featuring the dove—a universal symbol of peace. The following recipe can be modified to work with turkey for those of us not wanting to eat such an innocent-seeming bird.
(*Catching Fire*, Chapter 2)

Yields 4 servings

6 strips bacon

16 dove breast halves

1 cup seasoned flour, 3 tablespoons reserved (see Mrs. Everdeen's Rabbit Stew in Chapter 3 for recipe)

1½ cups heavy cream

1 tablespoon Italian parsley, chopped

Tips from Your Sponsor

During food shortages, it's likely President Snow would use pigeons in place of doves as they're basically interchangeable. The best part of the meat of these majestic creatures would be their breast, as that's really the only part of the bird that has any usable meat. Quail is also a suitable substitute for dove, though for every two dove breasts you only need one quail.

1. Fry bacon in a heavy skillet until crisp. Remove bacon and set aside. Keep bacon fat hot over medium-high heat.

2. Dredge dove breasts in seasoned flour and brown in the bacon fat for about 1 minute per side. Reduce heat and continue to cook until tender, for about 8–10 minutes. Set aside and cover with foil to keep warm.

3. Discard all but 3 tablespoons of the bacon drippings. Add the reserved 3 tablespoons of seasoned flour and stir to combine over medium heat.

4. Slowly stir in the cream and continue to cook over medium heat until smooth and thick. Add the dove breasts to the sauce to warm again. Serve four breasts per plate and garnish with chopped parsley.

FALL-OFF-THE-BONE TENDER DUCK

This is one of the meals Katniss's mother would prepare for the family after Katniss spent a day out studying nature while hunting with her father. The Everdeen family likely shared many laughs over this delicious dish; memories that Katniss can cling to during many a dark day.
(*Catching Fire*, Chapter 3)

Yields 6–8 servings

3 mallard ducks (6–7 pounds of duck)

3 tablespoons kosher salt, plus kosher salt and freshly ground black pepper to taste

2 apples, quartered

1 orange, quartered

1 cup orange juice

¼ cup dark honey

¼ cup pineapple juice

1 tablespoon Worcestershire sauce

2 tablespoons unsalted butter

2 tablespoons all-purpose flour

Tips from Your Sponsor

Properly cleaned ducks are the difference between an inedible and divine meal. When your fresh duck arrives, take time to go over each bird, fine cleaning the inside cavity and picking any stray feathers that didn't get plucked. Some of the fine hairs can be singed off with a lighter flame. Soak the bird in a big bowl of water and rinse. Do this several times until the water is clear. Then place duck in a bowl of salted water, about 2 or 3 tablespoons salt per gallon of water, for about 30 minutes.

1. Place ducks in a stockpot and cover with water. Add 3 tablespoons salt, apples, and orange, and bring to a boil. Cook for 45 minutes. Remove ducks and fruits from water and place in a pan, with fruits covering the duck.

2. Preheat the oven to 375°F. Combine orange juice, honey, pineapple juice, and Worcestershire sauce. Baste duck with sauce and place duck in oven for 30 minutes, uncovered.

3. Liberally baste with sauce again and add ½ cup to 1 cup water to pan to prevent sticking. Cover the pan tightly with a lid or cover tightly with heavy-duty foil.

4. Lower heat to 275°F. Roast for 2½–3 hours more, depending on size of ducks, basting with pan juices every 30 minutes. Add water to bottom of pan if dry. Ducks are done when leg joint falls apart.

5. To make gravy, after the ducks are removed from the pan add 2 tablespoons butter and 2 tablespoons flour to pan juices and cook until slightly thickened.

BANQUET BAKED PARTRIDGE WITH CREAM SAUCE

Game birds are regularly served at banquets at the Capitol, and this baked partridge is a likely offering. (*Catching Fire*, Chapter 6)

Yields 4 servings

2 partridges, approximately 2½ pounds each

1 cup flour

½ teaspoon kosher salt

2 teaspoons freshly ground black pepper

1 teaspoon dried thyme

1 teaspoon dried tarragon

¼ cup vegetable oil

3 tablespoons unsalted butter

2 cups heavy cream

1 cup chicken stock

Tips from Your Sponsor

English and French partridges are the most popular types of partridge for cooking. The common English grey partridge has a more subtle and delicate flavor than its larger, French counterpart. Both, however, are best served when younger in age. The older the bird, the tougher the meat.

1. Preheat oven to 325°F. Cut partridge into serving pieces, as you would chicken. Rinse thoroughly and pat dry.

2. Mix flour, salt, pepper, thyme, and tarragon in a large Ziploc bag. Place several partridge pieces at a time in the flour mixture and shake to coat with seasoned flour. Save the flour mixture.

3. In a large, heavy skillet, heat oil and butter at medium–high. Brown partridge pieces, approximately 5–6 minutes per side. Place the drumsticks, thighs, and wings into a large Dutch oven. Place the breasts on top of the dark meat.

4. Add ¼ cup of the dredging flour to the remaining oil and butter in the skillet. Cook over medium heat for 2 minutes. Slowly add the cream and chicken stock and cook for about 8–10 minutes or until mixture begins to bubble and thicken. Pour the cream sauce over the partridge.

5. Bake the partridge in the oven for 1–1½ hours or until meat is tender when pierced with a fork. (Longer baking time will be required for older birds.) Remove partridge pieces to warmed platter and serve.

DUCK WITH ORANGE SAUCE

One of the dishes Katniss most enjoys during the Capitol's banquet is this duck with orange sauce. It's not surprising that this dish is served, as oranges can represent prosperity—an idea that goes hand-in-hand with the Capitol.
(*Catching Fire*, Chapter 6)

Yields 1 Duck, or 6–8 servings

1 (12-ounce) can orange soda

1 (6-ounce) can frozen orange juice concentrate, thawed

1 (12-ounce) jar orange marmalade

1 cup honey barbecue sauce

½ cup brown sugar

¼ cup teriyaki sauce

1 teaspoon ginger

1 tablespoon honey

2 tablespoons lemon juice

1 (5-pound) whole duck, washed and excess fat removed

5 medium-sized oranges, peeled and sliced

Tips from Your Sponsor

Not in the mood for a whole duck? Try quartering this recipe with a teal, a small duck that weighs in at just 5–8 ounces after cleaning. Teal are said to be so delicious that it's hard to eat just one, so perhaps it's best to prepare a couple on the off chance that you or your guests will be hungrier than expected!

1. Pour the orange soda, orange concentrate, orange marmalade, barbecue sauce, brown sugar, teriyaki sauce, ginger, honey, and lemon juice into a large bowl. Stir until sugar is dissolved.

2. Preheat oven to 350°F. Place duck in a roasting pan. Using a fork, prick the skin of the duck all over to allow fat to drain off during roasting.

3. Brush the duck with the orange mixture. Place the oranges in the cavity of the duck, and spoon in some of the orange sauce.

4. Roast the duck in the preheated oven, brushing every 20 minutes with the orange sauce, until a meat thermometer inserted into the thigh of the duck reads at least 165°F, about 2½ hours.

CREAMED GOOSE OVER CRUMBLED BACON POLENTA

No Capitol banquet is complete without several fancy fowl dishes. Even the evil President Snow would want to stop to enjoy this delicious goose with bacon polenta, though it may be too rich for Katniss's tastes.
(*Catching Fire*, Chapter 6)

Yields 4 servings

4 tablespoons (½ stick) unsalted butter

2 cups fresh corn kernels (about 2 to 3 ears)

1 cup onion, chopped

2 tablespoons all-purpose flour

1½ cups half-and-half

2 cups cooked goose, chopped

1 cup grape tomatoes, halved

1 tablespoon tarragon, freshly chopped

Kosher salt and freshly ground pepper to taste

4 cups chicken stock

½ teaspoon kosher salt

1 cup cornmeal

½ cup Romano cheese, grated

6 slices crisp cooked bacon, crumbled

¼ cup parsley, finely chopped

1. Melt butter in a large skillet and sauté corn and onion for about 4–5 minutes. Stir in flour and heat for another 4–5 minutes. Continue to stir until bubbly. Slowly pour in half-and-half, whisking to blend. Cook until thickened and bubbling.

2. Add goose, tomatoes, and tarragon to sauce. Season to taste with salt and pepper. Simmer over low heat to keep warm.

3. To make polenta, bring chicken stock to a boil over high heat. Sprinkle in ½ teaspoon salt. Slowly sprinkle in the cornmeal, stirring to blend. Lower heat and cook until thickened, stirring occasionally. Remove from heat. Stir in cheese and bacon.

4. Spoon polenta into a shallow bowl and top with the creamy goose mixture. Garnish with chopped parsley.

Tips from Your Sponsor

Cooked until it's mush, polenta can be served with just a bit of butter, salt, and pepper for breakfast. Add Parmesan or Gorgonzola and let it sit to harden and it becomes perfect to slice into squares to either fry or grill.

ROAST PARTRIDGE AND WARM PEAR SALSA

It's likely that even the exotic and expensive partridge would have more than one offering at the Banquet. The warm, tangy pear salsa here complements the earthy partridge.
(*Catching Fire*, Chapter 6)

Yields 4–6 servings

> Roast Partridge:

2 whole partridges split in half

3 tablespoons extra-virgin olive oil

2 onions, sliced

8 garlic cloves, halved

½ cup white wine vinegar

½ cup white grape juice

¼ cup ginger ale

¼ cup orange juice

1 bay leaf

Kosher salt and freshly ground black pepper to taste

> Pear Salsa:

4 tablespoons (½ stick) unsalted butter

2 ripe pears, peeled and sliced

¼ cup golden raisins

¼ cup toasted walnuts

2 teaspoons fresh lime juice

1 teaspoon red pepper flakes

3 ounces Gorgonzola cheese

1. In a large skillet, brown partridge in the oil over high heat. Remove to a platter. Add the onions and garlic to the skillet and sauté for about 5 minutes, until garlic is lightly browned.

2. In a small bowl, mix together the white wine vinegar, grape juice, ginger ale, and orange juice.

3. Add the grape juice mixture to the onion and garlic sauté. Add bay leaf and bring to a boil. Add partridge and season to taste with salt and pepper. Cover and lower heat to a simmer. Cook for about 1 hour or until meat is tender.

4. Just before serving, prepare the pear salsa: In a small skillet, melt the butter. Add the sliced pears, golden raisins, and walnuts; sauté for 4–5 minutes.

5. Plate partridge and salsa. Sprinkle the lime juice and red pepper flakes over all. Crumble Gorgonzola cheese on top of salsa. Serve ½ partridge with ¼ of the salsa per person.

Tips from Your Sponsor

Partridges are best served in October when they are still full of grains from the fields. If lacking partridge, substitute with pheasant.

GOLDEN BANQUET GOOSE

If the Creamed Goose over Crumbled Bacon Polenta recipe is too rich for you, try this simple but nevertheless delicious golden goose!
(*Catching Fire*, Chapter 6)

Yields 8–10 servings

1 (8–10 pound) goose

Kosher salt and freshly ground black pepper to taste

2 onions, 1 sliced and 1 chopped

4 strips bacon

4 large carrots, chopped

2 cloves garlic, minced

2 teaspoons dried thyme

2 teaspoons dried tarragon

6 tablespoons butter

1¼ cups flour

3 (14.5-ounce) cans beef broth

1 (14.5-ounce) can tomatoes, chopped

1–2 cups white grape juice

Tips from Your Sponsor

Be careful when removing goose from the oven, as the bird is naturally fatty and there tends to be a lot of oil splatter. The fat that seeps to the bottom of the pan is tasty liquid gold. Try roasting potatoes with garlic in the goose fat for a superb side dish!

1. Preheat oven to 400°F. Rinse goose well; pat dry. Thoroughly sprinkle and rub salt and pepper inside and out. Place the slices of onion on the bottom of a roasting pan, then set the goose on the onions. Set aside.

2. In a large pot, fry the bacon until crisp. Remove the bacon to drain; reserve. Add the chopped onion and carrots to the bacon grease in the pan and sauté for about 5 minutes. Add the garlic, thyme, and tarragon and sauté for another 2–3 minutes.

3. Add the butter to the pot and allow to melt. Slowly stir in the flour to form a roux. Then slowly add the beef broth, whisking to avoid any lumps.

4. Add the tomatoes and 1 cup white grape juice to the sauce. Crumble the bacon and add it to the pot.

5. Bring the sauce to a boil and then reduce to a simmer. Season to taste with salt and pepper. Continue to simmer the sauce while the goose roasts. If sauce gets too thick, add another cup of white grape juice.

6. Place goose in the hot oven and roast uncovered for 20–30 minutes. Reduce heat to 325°F. Pour 2 cups of sauce over the goose. Cover tightly and roast for about 3 hours or more. Baste every 25 minutes, adding additional sauce if needed. Uncover the goose for the last 15–30 minutes for goose to brown.

7. Goose is done when legs move easily when wiggled. Serve with the sauce on the side.

TURKEY JERKY

While meat is not exactly plentiful in District 12, the wild turkey Katniss hunts can last the longest in jerky form. Finding ways to preserve what little they have is a necessary lesson for those who live in the District.
(*Catching Fire*, Chapter 7)

Yields 8–10 dozen strips

1 whole turkey breast, cut into very thin strips

4 tablespoons sugar

3 tablespoons seasoned salt

3 tablespoons seasoned pepper

1 tablespoon garlic salt

1 teaspoon red pepper flakes

2 tablespoons liquid smoke, hickory flavored

2 tablespoons Worcestershire sauce

1 cup water

Tips from Your Sponsor

The trick to cooking jerky in a relatively shorter amount of time has to do with how thin you cut the meat. Cut the strips very thin the first time you prepare this recipe. If cut thinly enough, it will cook in less than a day. You can make thicker jerky; it will just take longer to cook.

1. Place turkey strips in a plastic container with a tight-fitting lid.

2. Combine the sugar, salt, 1½ tablespoons of the seasoned pepper, garlic salt, red pepper flakes, liquid smoke, Worcestershire sauce, and water. Pour over turkey. Cover and refrigerate a day and a half (about 36 hours). Turn the container to mix the marinade several times.

3. When ready to cook, preheat oven to 150°F.

4. Line several baking trays with parchment paper. Remove turkey strips from marinade (discard marinade) and pat dry. Place on parchment-lined baking trays and sprinkle with the remaining 1½ tablespoons seasoned pepper.

5. Loosely crumple some aluminum foil for air circulation and place on oven racks. Set baking trays on foil. Bake for 10–20 hours or more, rotating baking trays every 6 hours.

MONTEREY JACK CHEESE, BACON, AND GREEN CHILI STUFFED TURKEY BREASTS

Not all turkey can be turned into turkey jerky. In a perfect world, Katniss and Peeta could cook their catch into a delicious, decadent dish such as this one. Like their friendship, this turkey dish is full of flavors and packs quite a punch.
(*Catching Fire*, Chapter 7)

Yields 4–6 servings

2 (2-pound) turkey breast halves

4 whole mild green chilies (canned)

8 ounces Monterey jack cheese, cut into 8 slices

4 bacon strips, cooked crisp

5 tablespoons extra-virgin olive oil

Kosher salt and freshly ground black pepper to taste

Tips from Your Sponsor

Not a fan of Monterey Jack cheese? Try Brie with sun-dried tomatoes and fresh basil leaves, or white Cheddar cheese with apricot preserves and chopped fresh rosemary.

1. Preheat oven to 350°F.

2. Slice a pocket in each turkey breast half. Slit open each green chili and place 2 slices of the cheese and a piece of crisp bacon inside. Insert 2 chilies in each turkey breast half. Slit the breast open a little more if needed, but do not cut all the way through. Close turkey breasts and secure with toothpicks.

3. Place turkey breasts in a greased, broiler-safe baking dish. Lightly coat turkey breasts with the olive oil. Season to taste with salt and pepper. Bake, covered, for half an hour or until the thickest part of the meat (and *not* the chilies) registers 160°F.

4. Uncover turkey breasts, drizzle with more olive oil, and broil for about 5 minutes until brown. Let rest for about 5 minutes. Then slice on the diagonal and serve.

ROAST PHEASANT

After enduring a grueling prep session where Flavius, Venia, and Octavia kept bursting into tears, Katniss is at her wits' end when she comes to lunch a few days before her re-entry into the Hunger Games. Luckily, this roast pheasant and its delicious side dishes, not to mention Cinna's good cheer, help to put Katniss in a somewhat better mood—not surprising due to the pheasant's traditional association with strength and courage. (*Catching Fire*, Chapter 15)

Yields 4 servings

2 pheasants (2½ pounds each)

2 oranges, halved

Kosher salt and freshly ground black pepper to taste

1 apple, quartered

1 onion, quartered

2 bay leaves

2 sprigs rosemary

2 tablespoons olive oil

8 slices bacon

1 cup chicken bouillon

½ cup apple cider

Jewel-Colored Mint Jelly (Chapter 4)

Tips from Your Sponsor

When roasting a pheasant, the breast meat gets done before the legs can get tender. So cut off the legs and place in the pan juices, covered, and cook for an additional 30–60 minutes or until the meat falls off the bone. Keep the breast meat warm or reheat in the oven just before serving.

1. Preheat oven to 350°F.

2. Rinse and dry pheasants. Squeeze oranges all over birds and inside the cavities. Season with salt and pepper. Place 1 half-squeezed orange, 2 apple quarters, 2 onion quarters, 1 bay leaf, and 1 sprig of rosemary in each cavity. Brush each bird with 1 tablespoon olive oil.

3. Place the pheasants in roasting pan and lay 4 slices of bacon over the breast of each bird. Pour the bouillon and apple cider into the pan.

4. Bake for 1½ hours, basting every 20 minutes with pan juices. Remove bacon and cook for another 15–20 minutes to brown the breast a bit. Pheasant is done when a meat thermometer registers 160–170°F in the breast.

5. Serve carved meat along with bowls of pan drippings and Jewel-Colored Mint Jelly.

KISS OF SMOKE BRIE-STUFFED PHEASANT BREAST

The Capitol is all about embellishment, whether it be embellishing the truth in their favor or putting together a "simple" dinner. When Katniss is served lunch, it's likely that there are multiple pheasant dishes—the previous roast pheasant dish, for example, and this more luxurious one. In the Capitol, it's nearly impossible to go hungry . . . or have a conscience.
(*Catching Fire*, Chapter 15)

Yields 4 servings

4 boneless, skinless pheasant breast halves (chicken is an acceptable substitution)

8 ounces Brie, sliced into 15–20 small slices

8 basil leaves

4 slices prosciutto

2 tablespoons olive oil

Tips from Your Sponsor

Most gas or charcoal grills come with directions for smoking or indirect cooking. Every unit is different, so follow the manufacturer's directions. Simple smoking is attained by cooking indirectly from the heat source.

1. Prepare a water smoker by adding 3 or 4 chunks of water-soaked wood (like oak, apple, or pecan) to the fire (see sidebar). Maintain a 225°F temperature during the smoking.

2. Flatten pheasant breasts with a meat mallet until ½" thick. Place 5 slices of Brie and 2 basil leaves in the middle of each flattened breast. Fold the sides over to enclose the cheese, tucking a little bit of the ends inward, too. Wrap a slice of prosciutto around each rolled breast. Lightly coat rolls with olive oil.

3. Place meat on aluminum pan and set in the smoker. Close lid and smoke for about 45–55 minutes. Pheasant is done when internal temperature is about 160–165°F. Remove from smoker and let rest for 10 minutes.

4. Serve the stuffed breast by slicing into ¾" slices to show off the stuffing.

PHEASANT BREAST MORNAY

Another pheasant dish likely served to Katniss in the Capitol is this Pheasant Breast Mornay. This dish is a richer and creamier offering than the Roast Pheasant recipe.
(*Catching Fire*, Chapter 15)

Yields 4 servings

4 tablespoons extra-virgin olive oil

4 boneless, skinless pheasant breast halves

1 cup seasoned flour, 4 tablespoons reserved (see Mrs. Everdeen's Rabbit Stew in Chapter 3 for recipe)

4 tablespoons (½ stick) unsalted butter

1 cup milk

1¼ cups Parmesan cheese, freshly grated

1/3 cup chopped Italian parsley to garnish

Tips from Your Sponsor

Mornay sauce is velvety and creamy. It goes well with any poultry and fish or shellfish. Chicken or fish stock can be added as part of the liquid to complement what is being served.

1. Preheat oven to 350°F. Lightly grease a baking dish and set aside.

2. Heat oil in a large skillet. Dredge pheasant breasts in ¾ cup seasoned flour and sauté until brown, about 4 minutes per side. Place breasts in oiled baking dish and place in the oven. Lay a piece of foil on top of baking dish but do not crimp or cover tightly. Bake for about 15 minutes or until meat is cooked through.

3. While pheasant is baking, melt the butter in a saucepan. Stir in the remaining 4 tablespoons of seasoned flour, and cook over medium heat to lightly brown the roux and incorporate the flour. Slowly add the milk, stirring over medium heat until thickened. Stir in cheese.

4. To serve, place the pheasant on a plate, spoon 2 tablespoons sauce over each breast, and sprinkle with parsley. Serve the remaining sauce on the side.

Plutarch Heavensbee enjoys a turkey leg while watching the tributes of the 75th Hunger Games train for battle. Now that he's the powerful new Head Gameskeeper, it's no wonder that Plutarch is depicted eating turkey, a bird that represents prosperity and abundance.
(*Catching Fire*, Chapter 16)

Yields 8–10 servings

1 (12–14-pound) wild turkey

½ cup (1 stick) unsalted butter, softened

2 tablespoons fresh thyme, chopped

1 clove garlic, minced

Zest of 1 lemon, inner fruit reserved

Kosher salt and freshly ground pepper to taste

8 bacon strips

Tightly woven cheesecloth

¼ cup extra-virgin olive oil

Tips from Your Sponsor

Wild turkey is a lean bird and tends to dry out rather quickly. Placing an herbed compound butter in between the skin and meat—a method called "larding"—covering the top with bacon, and then covering with oiled or buttered cheesecloth, is a triple precaution to help produce a moist, juicy bird.

1. Preheat oven to 325°F.

2. Rinse turkey and pat dry.

3. Combine butter, thyme, garlic, lemon zest, and salt and pepper to taste. Carefully spread the butter mixture between the skin and meat of the turkey, trying not to tear the skin.

4. Sprinkle the cavity of the bird with salt and pepper. Cut the lemon in half and place both halves in the cavity. Truss the legs and place the turkey in a roasting pan. Lay bacon strips over turkey.

5. Soak a 15" length of cheesecloth in the olive oil and place on top of the turkey. Roast turkey for about 10–12 minutes per pound. Baste with pan juices every 20–30 minutes. Remove cheesecloth and bacon for the last 10–15 minutes of cooking to allow bird to brown. Cook until the internal temperature is about 170°F when meat thermometer is inserted into the meaty part of the breast. The internal temperature will continue to rise another 5 degrees Fahrenheit while the turkey is resting.

6. Remove from oven. Let meat rest for 15 minutes before carving.

CHAPTER 7

PUT SOME MEAT ON YOUR BONES—BEEF, LAMB, AND PORK

The ever-vocal Katniss often manages to even use food to display her displeasure with the unfairness of the Hunger Games. When her voice has been diminished, she lets her actions speak for her. Whether she's shooting an arrow through Plutarch Heavensbee's Roasted Suckling Pig Surprise or snacking on Beef Strips from the Backpack, meats such as beef, lamb, and pork help Katniss get her opinions across loud and clear.

PLUTARCH HEAVENSBEE'S ROASTED SUCKLING PIG SURPRISE

One of Katniss's greatest traits is her ability to stand up for herself. She often does this without thinking first, but most of the time it gains her a lot of respect. When she's angry about the Gamekeepers focusing more on the roast pig than on her presentation, Katniss displays her usual impulsivity and shoots an arrow through the pig right in front of Plutarch Heavensbee and his cronies. Perhaps the pig represents Katniss's pigheadedness in the situation.
(*The Hunger Games*, Chapter 7)

Yields 1 suckling pig, or 8–10 servings

1 (15-pound) suckling pig
Kosher salt and fresh cracked black pepper

> Marinade:

¼ cup brown sugar

¾ cup garlic, chopped

¼ cup parsley, chopped

¼ cup fresh thyme, chopped

¼ cup oregano, chopped

3 bay leaves

3 tablespoons cumin

2 tablespoons paprika

2 cups onions, chopped

8 oranges, halved

4 limes, halved

4 lemons, halved

1 cup extra-virgin olive oil

1½ cups fresh pink grapefruit juice

> Stuffing:

1/3 cup vegetable oil

3 small onions, cut into tiny dice

3 garlic cloves, minced

1 large pineapple, peeled, cored, and cut into tiny dice

2 cups mango, cut into tiny dice

2 green apples, peeled, cored, and cut into tiny dice

2 Pink Lady apples, peeled, cored, and cut into tiny dice

4 large waxy potatoes, peeled and cut into tiny dice

¼ cup raisins

¼ cup macadamia nuts, chopped

2 tablespoons honey

3 tablespoons cinnamon

2 teaspoons nutmeg

2 teaspoons ground ginger

4 teaspoons ground allspice

6 fresh sage leaves, sliced

2 cups black beans, drained

Tips from Your Sponsor

WARNING: Properly roasting a suckling pig is a full two-day procedure. Make sure you have plenty of time (and that your oven is big enough for the pig).

1. Thoroughly clean the suckling pig. (Usually, you can get the butcher to do this for you.) Clean the inside and outside of the pig, and remove the eyeballs. Using a sharp knife, make several cuts in the pig's skin to stop it from bursting during cooking. Prop the pig's mouth open with a small apple.

2. Rub a good amount of salt and fresh cracked black pepper all over the suckling pig. Do not be afraid to get your hands dirty. Really season the pig.

3. Place the pig in a large heavy-duty garbage back and tightly tie closed. Place the pig in the refrigerator and chill for 12–15 hours.

4. Remove pig from fridge and thoroughly wash it with cold water.

5. In a mixing bowl, combine the marinade ingredients. Mix thoroughly. Season with more salt and pepper.

6. Place pig back in trash bag. Place another heavy-duty trash bag around the original trash bag (and pig). Pour the marinade over the pig, being sure to cover all of the pig with marinade. Tie both bags tightly and place the pig back in the refrigerator.

7. Refrigerate pig for another 12–15 hours, turning it every 3 hours.

8. About an hour before removing pig from the fridge, make the stuffing: Using a deep skillet, heat the vegetable oil at medium-high heat. Add the onions and garlic and cook for 3–5 minutes, stirring until slightly translucent. Reduce the heat to medium. Add the rest of the ingredients except the black beans, stirring thoroughly to evenly distribute the spices. Cook uncovered for 20–25 minutes, stirring often. Add the black beans. Let the mixture cool to room temperature.

9. Preheat oven to 350°F. Remove the pig from the fridge and the bags. Save the marinade.

10. Stuff the inside cavity of the pig with the stuffing. Using a kitchen needle and thread, tie up the cavity so stuffing won't escape during roasting. Tie the front legs and back legs. Cover tail with aluminum foil.

11. Place the pig in a large roasting pan and pour the saved marinade over the pig. Roast the pig in the preheated oven for 20 minutes per pound. Every hour, turn and baste the pig. Internal temperature should be around 160°F degrees before removing. Remove the pig from oven and allow it to rest for 45–60 minutes before slicing.

ROYAL RIB ROAST

Katniss might not realize it, but the thin slices of roast beef she enjoys during a Capitol dinner come from a well-cooked rib roast. The following recipe will make a bounty of sandwiches, or you can serve your roast with mashed potatoes and green beans for a homey and fulfilling dinner.
(*The Hunger Games*, Chapter 6)

Yields 1 Roast

1 (5-pound) standing beef rib roast

½ cup extra-virgin olive oil

3 teaspoons kosher salt

1 teaspoon fresh ground black pepper

½ teaspoon fresh ground red pepper

1 teaspoon rosemary

2 teaspoons garlic powder

1 teaspoon paprika

Tips from Your Sponsor

No matter how curious you may be, *do not open the oven*. Opening the oven door for even half a second will allow the heat that is necessary for a moist and delicious roast to escape. Every bit of heat is valuable!

1. Allow roast to stand at room temperature for at least 1 hour. Spread the olive oil evenly over roast, thoroughly coating it.

2. Preheat oven to 375°F. In a small bowl, mix salt, peppers, rosemary, garlic powder, and paprika together.

3. Place roast on a rack in a roasting pan fatty-side up, rib-side down. Rub the seasoning all over the roast, using all the seasoning.

4. Roast in oven for 1 hour. Turn the oven off and leave the roast inside to continue cooking. Do NOT open the door. Leave the roast in closed oven for 3 hours. Thirty minutes before serving, with oven door still closed, turn the temperature back up to 375°F to reheat the roast. When done, the internal temperature of the meat should be 145°F. Remove roast from the oven and let rest for 10 minutes before carving.

BREADED ITALIAN PORK CHOPS FOR THE BRAVE

After Katniss's private session with the Gamemakers, Haymitch attempts to make Katniss feel better with a lighthearted laugh. But although Haymitch chuckles and chows down on this pork chop—which represents his approval of Katniss's pigheadedness—Effie is horrified.
(*The Hunger Games*, Chapter 8)

Yields 4 servings

1 cup all-purpose flour

3 teaspoons kosher salt

2 teaspoons freshly grated pepper

2 eggs, lightly beaten

3 tablespoons milk

2 tablespoons Italian seasoning

1½ cups Italian seasoned bread crumbs

½ cup grated fresh Parmesan cheese

2 tablespoons dried basil

2 tablespoons rosemary

2 teaspoons kosher salt

4 tablespoons extra-virgin olive oil

4 cloves garlic, peeled and chopped

4 pork chops

Tips from Your Sponsor

For the juiciest of pork chops, ask your butcher for rib chops. Rib chops are located at the rib end of the loin and though they contain some fat, they are very tender and very flavorful. Though pricier, you will taste a definite difference between rib chops and the average, cheaper chop.

1. Preheat oven to 325°F.

2. Combine flour, 3 teaspoons salt, and pepper in a medium-sized bowl. In a small bowl, beat together eggs, milk, and Italian seasoning. In another small bowl, combine the bread crumbs, Parmesan cheese, basil, rosemary, and 2 teaspoons salt.

3. Heat the olive oil in a large cast-iron skillet over medium heat. Stir in the garlic, and cook until lightly browned. Remove garlic.

4. Dredge individual pork chops in flour mixture. Then dip each pork chop into the egg mixture. Finally, dip each flour-and-egg-coated pork chop into the bread-crumb mixture, coating evenly. Place coated pork chops in the skillet, and brown about 5 minutes on each side.

5. Place the skillet and pork chops in the preheated oven. Bake 25 minutes, or to an internal temperature of 160°F.

BEEF STRIPS FROM THE BACKPACK

Katniss finds beef jerky in the backpack that she grabs at the beginning of the 74th Hunger Games. This dried meat reinforces the fact that Katniss hasn't been able to find any water and feels pretty dried up herself. (*The Hunger Games*, Chapter 11)

Yields 6–8 servings

2 pounds flank steak

¼ cup soy sauce

3 tablespoons Worcestershire sauce

2 teaspoons Tabasco sauce

3 tablespoons honey

2 tablespoons liquid smoke

5 tablespoons brown sugar

1 tablespoon salt

2 teaspoons ground black pepper

1 teaspoon meat tenderizer

1 teaspoon garlic powder

2 teaspoons onion powder

2 teaspoons paprika

Tips from Your Sponsor

There are myriad ways to prepare jerky, from baking in the sun or oven to smoking it hot or cold. The trick is to get the moisture out of the meat so that it stores at room temperature in plastic bags or glass jars for many months.

1. Trim the flank steak of any excess fat, place meat in a Ziploc bag, and put it in the freezer 1–2 hours in order to firm up.

2. Remove the steak from the freezer and thinly slice the meat with the grain, into long strips.

3. Place beef strips in the bottom of a large bowl. Pour remaining ingredients over beef. Mix to assure all the meat is evenly coated. Cover and marinate in the refrigerator for at least 8 hours, or overnight.

4. Remove meat from the bowl, allowing marinade to drain off (discard remaining marinade). Place meat strips between two pieces of plastic wrap; pound to 1/8" thickness.

5. Arrange the meat strips on the tray of a dehydrator and dry at the dehydrator's highest setting until done to your liking, at least 4 hours.

6. Make sure the jerky has thoroughly cooled before storing. Airtight containers are your best bet, as moisture spoils the jerky.

CHAPTER 8

WILD GAME FOR WILD GIRLS

Unlike those in the Capitol who are helpless when trouble strikes, Katniss, Gale, Rue, and even Finnick are able to keep themselves alive by hunting. But this type of self-sufficiency comes down to more than just a class struggle or survival instinct. It also hints at the character of the people who later become key players in the rebellion. In The Hunger Games trilogy, as in life, you are what you eat. And the rebels in the trilogy who are able to thrive in the wilderness are all a little wild themselves; they're able to stand up in the face of adversity and they do things that others would be afraid to even try. So when you're sitting down for some Small Critter Casserole or taking a bite of Fightin' Fried Squirrel, don't be afraid if you start to feel a little daring. It comes with the territory.

SMALL CRITTER CASSEROLE

This recipe is easily adaptable for the many families living in the Seam who have to make do with whatever wild meat (rats, squirrels) they can find. Greasy Sae could also utilize this recipe when she's not in the mood for stew.
(*The Hunger Games*, Chapter 1)

Yields 8 servings

2 pounds small game meat, cut into 2" chunks

1 cup seasoned flour (see Mrs. Everdeen's Rabbit Stew in Chapter 3 for recipe)

¼ cup vegetable oil, more if needed

1 cup fresh broccoli

1 cup fresh green beans

½ cup fresh mushrooms

1½ cups artichoke hearts, chopped

8–10 green onions, chopped

2 cups chicken stock

1 12-ounce can cream of celery soup

2 tablespoons fresh thyme, chopped

Juice of one fresh lemon

Kosher salt and freshly ground pepper to taste

Tips from Your Sponsor

Serve this dish over egg noodles or cooked rice. If you want some extra zip in your casserole, add a pinch or two of red pepper flakes!

1. Dredge meat in seasoned flour and brown in a skillet with ¼ cup vegetable oil. Brown in two separate batches so the pan is not overcrowded. Add more oil if needed.

2. Return all browned meat to the skillet. Add broccoli, green beans, mushrooms, artichoke hearts, green onions, chicken stock, and celery soup. Cook over medium-high heat, stirring occasionally, until it just comes to a boil, about 12–15 minutes. Lower heat to a simmer, cover, and cook until meat is tender. Add thyme and lemon juice. Season to taste with salt and pepper.

3. Serve from the pot or transfer to a pretty serving bowl to serve family-style at the dinner table.

WILD RACCOON SAUTÉED IN BACON DRIPPINGS

In the Seam the old saying "beggars can't be choosers" couldn't be more relevant. In a society where any food is good food, it's likely that few wild raccoons could pass by a family without being killed and served for dinner.
(*The Hunger Games*, Chapter 1)

Yields 4 servings

1 (3- to 4-pound) raccoon, cut into pieces

3 stalks celery, roughly chopped

1 onion, quartered

2 bay leaves

Kosher salt and freshly ground black pepper to taste

4 strips bacon, chopped

1 onion, slivered

1 green bell pepper, cut into strips

4 Roma tomatoes, chopped

½ cup apple juice

Tips from Your Sponsor

When it comes to wild game, the younger, smaller animals yield a tastier dish. Thus, raccoons are best when they weigh 6 pounds or less fully dressed.

1. Place raccoon meat in a large pot and fill to cover with water. Add celery, quartered onion, and bay leaves. Bring to a boil, then lower heat and simmer for one hour.

2. Remove meat from pot, let cool, and debone. Sprinkle meat with salt and pepper and set aside.

3. In a large skillet, sauté bacon and slivered onion until just beginning to brown. Add raccoon meat and sauté until lightly browned. Add pepper, tomatoes, and apple juice. Simmer for about 20–30 minutes, until meat is fork tender.

MR. MELLARK'S FAVORITE FRIED SQUIRREL

Peeta's father loves squirrel meat and often buys it from Katniss when his wife isn't around. That he buys squirrel is certainly appropriate; the squirrel is known to be an animal that hides its food from prying eyes.
(*The Hunger Games*, Chapter 4)

Yields 4–6 servings

2 squirrels, cut into pieces

2 cups seasoned flour (see Mrs. Everdeen's Rabbit Stew in Chapter 3 for recipe)

4 eggs

½ cup whole milk

1 cup vegetable oil for frying

Tips from Your Sponsor

The oil in your pan should be hot but not smoking. As pieces of food are placed in the skillet, the temperature of the oil will decrease. Adjusting the temperature is a must. So raise the heat before putting the meat in the hot oil, then lower it a smidge. Repeat with the next batch.

1. Clean and rinse pieces of meat. Place in a large pot and fill with salted water to cover. Refrigerate for 2 hours or overnight.

2. When ready to fry, remove from salted water and pat dry.

3. Place seasoned flour in a large bowl. In another large bowl, combine eggs and milk; beat well.

4. Dip each piece of meat first in the egg mixture and then in the flour mixture, then dip in the egg and flour again. Set on a platter.

5. In the meantime, heat the oil in a large skillet until hot. Fry several pieces of the meat at a time, making sure not to crowd the skillet. Fry meat, turning several times until meat is cooked through, tender, and golden brown, about 12–15 minutes for small pieces of meat and 16–18 minutes for larger pieces. Serve hot.

WILD SQUIRREL & SAUSAGE GUMBO

Sometimes Katniss shows her resourcefulness (another quality associated with the squirrel) by making squirrel stew. With or without the sausage, this gumbo would be a filling alternative—and one admired even by the opinionated Greasy Sae.
(*The Hunger Games,* Chapter 4)

Yields 8 servings

2–3 pounds squirrel

2 tablespoons extra-virgin olive oil

Kosher salt and freshly ground black pepper to taste

1 pound spicy Italian sausage, casings removed

4 tablespoons (½ stick) unsalted butter

2 onions, chopped

1 green bell pepper, chopped

4 stalks celery, chopped

½ pound fresh mushrooms, sliced

2 cloves garlic, minced

6 tablespoons all-purpose flour

8 cups chicken broth, divided

1 cup fire-roasted red pepper, chopped

½ teaspoon red pepper flakes

1 teaspoon dried thyme

2 bay leaves

Tips from Your Sponsor

Try this recipe with other small wild game such as rabbit, and beef consommé instead of chicken broth!

1. Preheat the oven to 400°F. Cut squirrel into pieces. Rub the meat with 2 tablespoons oil and season with salt and pepper. Place in a roasting pan and roast for about 45–60 minutes, or until tender. Remove, let cool, and pick the meat off the bones. Set aside.

2. Brown sausage in a large pot over medium-high heat. Add butter, onions, bell pepper, celery, mushrooms, and garlic. Sauté for about 10–12 minutes, stirring slowly.

3. Stir in flour to form a roux and cook for about 3–4 minutes. Slowly add 2 cups of the chicken broth, stirring to combine; add the rest of the broth, red pepper, fire-roasted red pepper flakes, thyme, bay leaves, and squirrel.

4. Bring the mixture to a gentle boil. Lower the heat and simmer, uncovered, for 2 hours. If mixture is too thick, add 1–2 cups of water or additional chicken broth. Season to taste with salt and pepper. Remove bay leaves before serving.

KATNISS'S COTTAGE PIE

Shepherd's pie, originally called cottage pie, earned its name when potatoes were introduced as an edible crop possible for the poor. In fact, in early variations of this recipe, any leftover meat could be used for the filling, and mashed potatoes served as the topping as well as the lining. This is the kind of hearty recipe that the Everdeens and all members of the Seam would likely attempt to make in an effort to stave off hunger. (*The Hunger Games*, Chapter 4)

Yields 6–8 servings

2 pounds ground sheep/mutton (or other big-game meat)

3–4 tablespoons extra-virgin olive oil

2 cloves garlic, minced

1 onion, chopped

1 red bell pepper, chopped

½ cup mushrooms, sliced

4 tablespoons (½ stick) unsalted butter

4 tablespoons all-purpose flour

2 cups chicken broth

2 teaspoons Worcestershire sauce

Kosher salt and fresh ground pepper to taste

1 (9") unbaked pastry crust

Tips from Your Sponsor

There are many possible toppings for a pot pie. While this recipe uses the traditional pastry crust, other topping choices include the aforementioned mashed potatoes, puffed pastry, buttered bread crumbs, and phyllo dough. Even biscuit dough makes a good topping. Try using the dough from Katniss-Approved Puffy Buttermilk Biscuits (Chapter 2).

1. Preheat oven to 450°F. Grease a 2-quart baking dish.

2. Sauté ground meat in 3 tablespoons olive oil until cooked through and browned. Transfer meat to baking dish. Add 1 more tablespoon of oil to pan if needed. Sauté garlic, onion, red bell pepper, and mushrooms until tender, 4–5 minutes. Spoon over meat in baking dish.

3. Pour off excess oil from pan. Melt butter and add flour to form a roux. Cook for about 3–4 minutes over medium-high heat. Slowly add the chicken broth, stirring to keep smooth. Cook until bubbly and slightly thickened.

4. Remove sauce from heat and add Worcestershire sauce. Season to taste with salt and pepper. Pour over meat and vegetables.

5. Roll out pastry crust to fit over casserole dish. Crimp edges to seal. Prick with a fork to allow steam to escape. Bake until crust is well browned, about 25–30 minutes. Serve hot.

RABBIT PIE WITH DROPPED HERBED ROLLS

One of Katniss's fondest memories is hunting with Gale, where they frequently bagged rabbits. She likely thinks of this particular animal based on its association with luck, which is exactly what she needs as she prepares to go into the arena.
(*The Hunger Games*, Chapter 8)

Yields 6 servings

> Rabbit Pie:

3 cups cooked rabbit, chopped

1 onion, chopped

4 tablespoons (½ stick) unsalted butter

½ cup fresh mushrooms, sliced

3 tablespoons all-purpose flour

2 cups chicken broth

½ cup fresh carrots, chopped

½ cup broccoli florets

4 small peeled red potatoes, halved

½ cup fresh green peas

Kosher salt and seasoned pepper to taste

> Dropped Herbed Rolls:

1 cup (2 sticks) unsalted butter, softened

2 cups self-rising flour

1 tablespoon sugar

1 cup sour cream

4 tablespoons fresh herbs, chopped (chives, parsley, tarragon, or thyme)

1. Preheat oven to 350°F. Butter a baking dish. Spread cooked rabbit in the dish.

2. Sauté onion in butter for 5 minutes. Add mushrooms and cook for an additional 5 minutes, stirring. Sprinkle with flour and stir to blend. Slowly add the chicken broth, stirring to combine.

3. Cook sauce until beginning to boil, stirring occasionally. Add carrots, broccoli, potatoes, and peas. If mixture seems too thick, add ¼–½ cup hot water. Season to taste with salt and pepper. Pour mixture over rabbit.

4. For rolls: In a large bowl, cut butter into flour and sugar. Stir in sour cream. Add the herbs. Drop by rounded spoonfuls over the rabbit pie.

5. Bake pie for 20–25 minutes, until mixture is bubbly and rolls are slightly brown.

Tips from Your Sponsor

This is a great way to use leftover rabbit or other small game. Feel free to use any vegetables desired in this pie, whether they be fresh, frozen, or from a jar or can. Try using cauliflower or even Brussels sprouts for a warm winter vegetable pie!

FRESHLY SNARED BARBECUED RABBIT

As the Hunger Games begin, Katniss has the foresight to make some rudimentary snares and immediately manages to catch "one fine rabbit." Quick like a bunny (pun intended), Katniss cleans and guts the animal and uses a dead tribute's fire to roast it. Lucky for us, we have an oven and spices, but this recipe will help give us a taste of the wild game Katniss was forced to survive on during the 74th Hunger Games. (*The Hunger Games*, Chapter 12)

Yields 4 servings

2 whole small rabbits, cut up in strips

2–3 tablespoons olive oil

4 tablespoons Spicy Chipotle Rub (see recipe)

2 cups barbecue sauce

3 cloves garlic, minced

1 ½ teaspoons toasted sesame oil

Spicy Chipotle Rub

¼ cup garlic powder

2 tablespoons dried ground chipotle

2 tablespoons ground allspice

2 tablespoons dark brown sugar

1 tablespoon dried ground cloves

1 tablespoon dried orange zest

1 tablespoon thyme

1 tablespoon dried cilantro

2 teaspoons onion salt

1 teaspoon red pepper flakes

Combine all the ingredients in a glass jar and cover with a tight-fitting lid. Keeps for up to 3 months.

1. Preheat oven to 350°F.

2. Lightly coat rabbit pieces with olive oil and sprinkle with the Spicy Chipotle Rub (or rub of your choice). Lay rabbit pieces in a single layer in a baking pan. Bake for 30 minutes.

3. Combine the barbecue sauce, garlic, and sesame oil. Liberally or to taste, brush sauce on meat. Continue to bake for 30–60 minutes or more, until meat is fork tender and pulling from the bone. Baste with additional barbecue sauce to taste.

SPICY WILD GROOSLING CHILI

While waiting to strike vengeance for Rue's murder, Katniss kills a flock of groosling—an act that mirrors the quick, cold way the boy from District 1 died. If Katniss had had time to focus on the groosling, perhaps she would have prepared this delicious chili.
(*The Hunger Games,* Chapter 18)

Yields 8–12 servings

2 pounds ground groosling (or wild turkey)

2 tablespoons olive oil

2 onions, chopped

4 cloves garlic, minced

2 teaspoons oregano

2 teaspoons cumin

2 (10-ounce) cans Ro-Tel Original Diced Tomatoes and Green Chilies

3 (15-ounce) cans cannellini beans

6 cups chicken broth

3 cups sharp Cheddar cheese, shredded

1 cup green onion, chopped

1 cup fresh jalapeño, seeded and chopped

1 cup fresh cilantro, chopped

Tips from Your Sponsor

Chili is always an excellent option for a dinner party. Try serving with blue corn tortilla chips or with Katniss-Approved Puffy Buttermilk Biscuits (Chapter 2)!

1. In a large pot, brown the ground groosling (or turkey) in oil, keeping the meat in small clumps rather than breaking it into fine pieces. Add the onions and garlic, cooking until soft. Add the oregano and cumin and mix well to blend. Then add the tomatoes, beans, and chicken broth. Simmer for about 1 hour.

2. When ready to serve, set up a garnishing station with a bowl of cheese, a bowl of green onion, a bowl of jalapeño, and a bowl of cilantro. Spoon up the bowls of chili and let everyone garnish to their own liking.

GRILLED VENISON CHOPS WITH BÉARNAISE BUTTER

Katniss remembers how she bought Prim her beloved (not to mention useful) goat with the money she earned by trading one of her first slain deer. Deer are gentle, watchful creatures, just like Katniss . . . even though she hides those traits from everyone but her little sister.
(*The Hunger Games*, Chapter 20)

Yields 4 servings

> Chops:

2 tablespoons olive oil

4 venison chops or steaks

2 tablespoons coarse kosher salt and freshly cracked pepper, combined

Béarnaise Butter to taste

> Béarnaise Butter:

½ cup (1 stick) softened unsalted butter

2 tablespoons shallots

1 tablespoon tarragon vinegar

1 tablespoon chopped fresh tarragon

½ tablespoon chopped fresh Italian parsley

¼ teaspoon kosher salt

¼ teaspoon hot sauce

Tips from Your Sponsor

Béarnaise butter is the child of Béarnaise sauce, a famous French sauce consisting of clarified butter emulsified in egg yolks and seasoned with herbs. It takes some chefs years to perfect their Béarnaise sauce, which is named after the Béarn region in southwestern France.

1. Prepare a hot fire in the grill.

2. Rub olive oil on meat and sprinkle with salt and pepper. Set aside.

3. Make the Béarnaise Butter by mixing all the ingredients together in a small serving bowl. Set aside.

4. Grill meat for about 3–4 minutes per side for rare to medium rare. Serve with a pat of the Béarnaise Butter on top.

VENISON, APPLE, AND CHEDDAR PUFF PASTRY

While this is a much fancier and intricate use of venison, even citizens of the Seam have to celebrate every once in a while. This is a delicious and relatively simple pastry recipe that works for any meal, whether it be breakfast, lunch, or dinner.
(*The Hunger Games*, Chapter 20)

Yields about 12 servings, or 2 pastries

½ pound ground venison

½ pound Italian sausage

1 large yellow onion, chopped

2 large tart apples, peeled, cored, and chopped

1 cup cooked wild rice

1 pound sharp Cheddar cheese

1 teaspoon kosher salt

½ teaspoon freshly cracked black pepper

2 eggs

1 tablespoon heavy cream

2 sheets frozen puff pastry, thawed

Tips from Your Sponsor

To prevent your puff pastry from getting soggy, you can sprinkle a bit of sugar and flour (equal parts of 1–2 tablespoons) on top of pastry crust before adding the filling. The egg and cream glaze, meanwhile, will give your pastry a nice golden-brown top.

1. Preheat oven to 400°F. Lightly butter two large baking sheets and set aside.

2. Brown meat in a skillet over medium-high heat. Add onion and cook until soft. Transfer meat mixture to a large bowl, draining off any liquid. Add apples, rice, cheese, salt, and pepper. Beat 1 of the eggs and stir into meat mixture to bind.

3. On a lightly floured work surface, roll out each of the 2 puff pastry sheets to a 14" x 18" rectangle. Spoon half of the mixture down the center of each rectangle, starting 3" from the bottom. Be sure to leave 3" from the top for folding. Fold the top and bottom edges of the pastry over the filling. Then cut the pastry remaining on either side of the filling into diagonal strips about ½" wide. Then make diagonal cuts about ½" apart in the pastry remaining on either side of the filling.

4. Braid the strips, alternately from each side, over the filling. Cut off any excess dough. Repeat with other pastry.

5. Place each pastry on a baking sheet. Beat the remaining egg with the 1 tablespoon cream and brush over both pastries. Bake for 30 minutes or until pastry is puffed and golden brown.

VENISON-STUFFED PEPPER BOATS

Last but not least, this spicy venison dish works as both an appetizer *or* an entrée.
(*The Hunger Games*, Chapter 20)

Yields 6 pepper boats

1 (6-ounce) package couscous

1 large red bell pepper

1 large yellow bell pepper

1 large green bell pepper

1 pound ground venison

1 cup onion, chopped

2 tablespoons olive oil

1½ cups spicy tomato juice

12 ounces feta cheese, crumbled and divided

1 cup kalamata olives, chopped

½ cup fresh Italian parsley, finely chopped

1 teaspoon seasoned black pepper

Tips from Your Sponsor

Lacking venison? Try this recipe with ground turkey breast for a healthier meal. Try mixing in minced garlic with the meat for extra spice.

1. Preheat oven to 350°F. Prepare couscous according to package directions. Place in large bowl.

2. Stem, seed, and halve bell peppers. Place the peppers skin-side down on a well-oiled baking pan.

3. Sauté venison and onion in olive oil until meat is browned and onion is soft. Add spicy tomato juice and heat until bubbling. Pour mixture into the bowl of couscous. Add 2/3 of the feta and all of the olives, parsley, and seasoned pepper, stirring to combine well.

4. Fill pepper halves evenly with the mixture. Top with the remaining crumbled feta cheese.

5. Bake for about 20–30 minutes. Serve as an appetizer or as a main course.

While Katniss hunts squirrels—an animal associated with practicality due to the fact that it saves its food to get through the harsh winter months—Peeta accidentally, and not-so-practically, gathers poisonous Nightlock berries. However, like the squirrels that she hunts, Katniss saves the berries and is able to use them during a harsh time in the arena.
(*The Hunger Games*, Chapter 23)

Yields 4 servings

1/3 cup all-purpose flour

1 teaspoon kosher salt

¼ teaspoon freshly ground black pepper

¼ teaspoon cayenne pepper

2 whole small squirrels, quartered

½ cup vegetable oil

1½ cups whole milk

Kosher salt and freshly ground black pepper to taste

Tips from Your Sponsor

Squirrels, like most wild game, come in varying sizes. Fox squirrels are larger than gray squirrels, weighing in at 1 pound dressed. Three will feed four people. The smaller grays weigh about ¾ pound dressed and feed one person each.

1. In a large Ziploc bag, combine flour, kosher salt, black pepper, and cayenne pepper. Shake to mix. Add squirrel pieces to bag and shake to coat.

2. In a large skillet, heat oil on medium-high heat until hot and bubbling. Add coated squirrel and brown on all sides. Reserve discarded bag of flour mixture.

3. Reduce heat and cover skillet. Cook on low heat until tender, about 40–45 minutes, turning pieces once about halfway through.

4. Remove cover; let meat cook for another 5 minutes to crisp. Transfer meat to a plate lined with paper towels. Set aside and keep warm.

5. Discard all but 2 tablespoons of oil. Over medium heat, stir flour mixture into reserved oil. Slowly pour in milk and cook over medium heat, stirring frequently, until the sauce thickens. Once bubbling, add salt and pepper to taste. Serve on top of squirrel.

HAZELLE'S BEAVER STEW WITH ROSEMARY POTATOES

Though Gale is forced to spend most of his time in the mines, Katniss manages to trap a beaver that Gale's mom Hazelle plans to turn into a nice stew. Here the beaver represents hard work and family, both of which Katniss thinks of whenever she speaks to Hazelle.
(Catching Fire, Chapter 1)

Yields 6–8 servings

> Stew:

1 (6 pound) beaver, cut into pieces

Water to cover

1 cup cider vinegar

1 cup seasoned flour

¼ cup vegetable oil

3 onions, quartered

3 cloves garlic, minced

3 carrots, peeled and chopped

3 golden potatoes, peeled and chopped

3 turnips, peeled and chopped

2 small butternut squash, peeled and chopped

2½ cups chicken broth, or more as needed

Kosher salt and freshly ground black pepper to taste

> Rosemary Potatoes:

2 pounds red potatoes, chopped

2 tablespoons chopped rosemary

1½ tablespoons garlic, minced

¼ teaspoon garlic salt

1½ teaspoons kosher salt

2 teaspoons fresh ground pepper

½ cup olive oil

Tips from Your Sponsor

Beaver is a rather gamy meat. Be sure to remove the fat from the beaver before cooking, as it has a strong odor—not to mention flavor—that can be quite off-putting. To draw out the excess blood, soak the beaver meat in salted water along with ¼ cup vinegar overnight in the refrigerator, then rinse the meat in cold, clear water.

> Stew:

1. Place beaver pieces in a large pot, cover with water, and add cider vinegar. Refrigerate for at least 12 hours or overnight.

2. Remove meat, pat dry, and dredge in seasoned flour. Place flour-coated meat on a large plate. Discard the water.

3. Heat the oil in a heavy pot or Dutch oven. Sauté meat in batches over medium-high to high heat until golden brown. Remove last batch of meat from the pot. Place onions and garlic on the bottom of the pot, and then lay all the meat over the onions.

4. Add carrots, potatoes, turnips, butternut squash, and chicken broth. Bring broth to boil. Reduce heat and simmer for 1½–2 hours or until meat is fork tender and vegetables are done. While the stew is cooking, make the Rosemary Potatoes.

> Rosemary Potatoes:

1. Preheat oven to 375°F. Oil a baking sheet.

2. In a large pot, boil potatoes until just tender; drain well.

3. Toss potatoes with remaining ingredients in a large bowl.

4. Transfer potatoes to the baking sheet and bake for 25–30 minutes, or until browned and fragrant.

5. Remove from oven. If desired, sprinkle additional coarse salt and rosemary over potatoes.

6. Season stew with salt and pepper to taste. Serve with the potatoes alongside or on a separate plate.

BANQUET-BAKED MOUNTAIN GOAT WITH ARTICHOKES, TOMATOES, AND FRESH HERBS

The roasting goats that Katniss sees at the banquet need to be turned into some form of a servable dish, and this recipe fits right in with the other decadent recipes that would likely be served at a Capitol function.
(*Catching Fire*, Chapter 6)

Yields 4 servings

2 pounds wild goat tenderloin or round steak

2 tablespoons extra-virgin olive oil

Kosher salt and freshly ground black pepper to taste

1 cup artichoke hearts

1 (28-ounce) can whole tomatoes

2 cloves garlic, minced

2 tablespoons fresh parsley, chopped

1 tablespoon fresh oregano, chopped

Zest and juice of 1 lemon

4–6 basil leaves, torn for garnish

Tips from Your Sponsor

Mountain goat is a strong-flavored animal. If too old, its meat will be tough and stringy. Only cook goat when you have access to young meat, or brine the older meat prior to cooking. Either way, a baked stew of sorts is an excellent way to get good results from this goat. Serve with cooked rice.

1. Preheat oven to 350°F.

2. Cut the meat into 1½" cubes. Coat with olive oil and salt and pepper to taste. Sauté for about 3–4 minutes, until lightly browned. Remove meat from skillet and place in a covered baking dish or Dutch oven.

3. Place artichokes and tomatoes in the skillet and heat until bubbling. Stir in the garlic, parsley, oregano, and lemon zest and juice. Season to taste with salt and pepper. Pour over the meat.

4. Bake, covered, for 45–60 minutes, until meat is fork tender. Garnish with torn basil leaves.

GAME BIRD BREASTS MARENGO

Another succulent wild bird recipe that would likely be offered at the banquet, this one uses bacon and tomatoes for a less creamy but nonetheless rich offering.
(*Catching Fire*, Chapter 6)

Yields 8 servings

1 pound bacon

8 boneless, skinless game bird breasts

1 ½ cups seasoned flour (see Mrs. Everdeen's Rabbit Stew in Chapter 3)

2 onions, chopped

3 cloves garlic, minced

3 (10-ounce) cans diced tomatoes and green chilies

1 pound fresh whole button mushrooms

½ cup parsley, chopped

Zest of 1 lemon

Tips from Your Sponsor

Ever wonder whether fresh tomatoes are better than canned ones? Let your taste buds guide you. Certainly, fresh summer tomatoes are best, but their season is not long. If you're weary of the quality of your local grocer's tomatoes, used canned ones, but choose a premium brand that is fire-roasted with bits of the charred skin still on the fruit. These are quite tasty.

1. Preheat oven to 350°F. Lightly grease a large, deep baking dish and set aside.

2. In a large sauté pan, fry bacon until crisp. Remove bacon to drain on paper towels. Leave the bacon grease in the pan. When the bacon is cool, crumble it and set aside.

3. Dredge game bird breasts in seasoned flour; save remaining flour. Brown breasts in bacon grease, cooking about 4 minutes per side. Place breasts in baking dish.

4. Pour off half of bacon grease remaining in the pan. Sauté chopped onions and garlic in grease until soft. Add ¼ cup of the seasoned flour used for dredging and stir to form a roux. Add tomatoes, mushrooms, half the parsley, lemon zest, and half the crumbled bacon. Heat to boiling, stirring constantly. If tomato gravy is too thick, thin with water.

5. Pour gravy over breasts and top with remaining bacon. Bake for approximately 1 hour. Sprinkle remaining parsley over game birds and serve.

GRILLED TREE RAT WITH PEANUT BUTTER DIPPING SAUCE

After Katniss catches some questionable meat they dub Tree Rat, Peeta shows that he's becoming more accustomed to improvisation when he roasts the chunks of tree rat in the Quarter Quell arena's force field.
(*Catching Fire*, Chapter 20)

Yields 4 servings

4 whole wild rats or squirrels, skinned and cut into pieces

Kosher salt and freshly ground black pepper to taste

Zest and juice of 1 lime

1/3 cup pineapple juice

1/3 cup heavy cream

¼ cup creamy peanut butter

¼ cup chili sauce

½ cup (1 stick) unsalted butter

Tips from Your Sponsor

While not common in North American households, eating rat is typical in areas of India, the Philippines, Thailand, Cambodia, and Ghana. In the United States, however, we're more likely to feed rats to our pet snakes than eat them ourselves.

1. Prepare a hot fire in the grill. Sprinkle rat pieces with salt and pepper to taste.

2. Combine lime zest and juice, pineapple juice, heavy cream, peanut butter, and chili sauce in a saucepan. Simmer for 10 minutes, stirring.

3. Melt butter in a saucepan and take out to the grill. Baste rats with butter and grill over medium-high heat for about 15–20 minutes or until leg meat pulls away from the bone.

4. Serve with individual bowls of peanut butter dipping sauce and plenty of hand towels.

75TH HUNGER GAMES' DUTCH OVEN TREE RAT

If Grilled Tree Rat with Peanut Butter Dipping Sauce doesn't sound good, try this dish for an even juicier meal. As brine is used to make a piece of meat even more moist and tender, this dish can't help be anything but. (*Catching Fire*, Chapter 20)

Yields 6–8 servings

1 (6- to 8-pound) tree rat (or muskrat), cut into pieces

Vinegar and Salt Brine (see recipe)

6 strips bacon, chopped

1 onion, sliced

1 cup seasoned flour (see Mrs. Everdeen's Rabbit Stew in Chapter 3)

1 cup beef consommé

1 cup sour cream

> **Vinegar and Salt Brine (2 quarts):**

1 quart water

3 cups cider vinegar

½ cup kosher salt

1/3 cup dark brown sugar

1 tablespoon black peppercorns

1 bunch Italian parsley, chopped

1 onion, chopped

2 carrots, chopped

2 stalks celery, chopped

Combine all of the ingredients in a pot and bring to a boil. Turn off heat and let cool. Strain the liquid and toss the vegetables. Brine the game of your choice for at least 12 hours and up to 3 days in the refrigerator.

1. Soak pieces of tree rat (or muskrat) in a large bowl of Vinegar and Salt Brine in refrigerator overnight.

2. Remove meat and throw brine away. Remove as much fat from meat as possible and set meat aside.

3. Fry chopped bacon in a Dutch oven until beginning to brown. Add onion and cook for 3–4 minutes.

4. Dredge meat in seasoned flour and brown over medium-high to high heat with the bacon and onion. Brown in two batches and avoid crowding the pan. Remove browned meat to a plate.

5. When meat is browned, place back in the pan. Add beef consommé and simmer for an hour until meat is fork tender. Add the sour cream and warm through.

CHAPTER 9

JUST DESSERTS

Desserts in The Hunger Games trilogy are a vivid reminder of the class struggle between the Districts and the Capitol. In the Capitol, not a meal goes by without a flashy and fantastic treat that is likely to send the diner straight into a sugar coma. Here decadence reigns supreme and, with food as with life, the Capitol's citizens expect to receive their just desserts. In the other Districts, however, desserts represent a small plate of hope; a bit of sweetness in a harsh world, which is exactly what Peeta, the baker, ends up being for Katniss. As you taste the treats in this chapter, take courage from the struggles of the Districts and don't be afraid to seek out sweetness in your own life.

CHOCOLATE-COVERED STRAWBERRIES

An easy dessert to make with the many fresh strawberries Katniss picks around District 12, these Chocolate-Covered Strawberries are a must for any berry-lover in possession of a sweet tooth. Additionally, strawberries are traditionally associated with desire and lust, so it's no surprise that they're mentioned the first time we see Katniss and Gale together.
(*The Hunger Games*, Chapter 1)

Yields 4 cups

8 ounces high-quality semisweet chocolate, chopped

8 ounces high-quality milk chocolate, chopped

8 ounces high-quality white chocolate, chopped

1 pound fresh strawberries (with stem), rinsed and dried

Tips from Your Sponsor

If possible, use chopped chocolate bars or chunks instead of chips. Chips are made with less cocoa butter which makes them harder to melt. Also, be careful not to let the boiling water touch the chocolate; it will cause your chocolate to seize up and thicken. If this happens, try adding a teaspoon of canola oil or warm water to the chocolate mixture and stir constantly until the chocolate smoothes.

1. Line one large metal cookie sheet with parchment paper. Chill the lined sheet in fridge for half an hour.

2. Place chopped semisweet and milk chocolates in one bowl and the white chocolate in a separate bowl. Using a double boiler, melt the semisweet and milk chocolate, stirring occasionally until mixture is smooth. If lacking a double boiler, melting chocolate in a bowl placed over hot water will do. Don't let the water touch the bottom of the upper pan. The chocolate mixture should actually be cool to the touch while melting.

3. Once chocolate is melted, remove from heat. Holding strawberries by the stem, dip the berries into semisweet and milk chocolate mixture, then place on chilled parchment-lined cookie sheet.

4. Repeat Step 3 using white chocolate. Spoon melted white chocolate into a small Ziploc bag. Cut corner off bag, and drizzle white chocolate over milk chocolate-covered strawberries.

5. Set strawberries aside to set at room temperature, at least one hour. Serve.

EVEN THE SEAM HAS SWEETS: BLACKBERRY COBBLER FOR SPECIAL DAYS

Gale jokingly wishes Katniss luck at the upcoming reaping for the 74th Hunger Games by tossing a blackberry at her. She enjoys its "sweet tartness" while simultaneously understanding the black humor that Gale is tossing her way.
(*The Hunger Games*, Chapter 1)

Yields 8 servings

1 cup all-purpose flour

2 teaspoons cinnamon

1 cup white sugar

1 teaspoon baking powder

1 teaspoon kosher salt

6 tablespoons unsalted butter, cold

1 teaspoon vanilla extract

¼ cup boiling water

2 tablespoons cornstarch

¼ cup cold water

½ cup turbinado sugar

2 tablespoons lemon juice

4 cups fresh blackberries, rinsed

Tips from Your Sponsor

Cobblers can be enjoyed in any form, whether blackberry or raspberry or blueberry or a mixture thereof! So, lacking blackberries? Try a blueberry cobbler. Or how about a Brown Betty, which is a silly name for a dessert made of bread crumbs (or graham cracker crumbs), sugar, spices, and fruit—commonly diced apples—alternately layered in a baking dish.

1. Preheat oven to 400°F. Line an 8" x 8" baking dish with foil.

2. To make dough for topping: In a large bowl, mix the flour, 1 teaspoon of the cinnamon, ½ cup of the white sugar, baking powder, and salt. Cut in the butter until the mixture resembles bread crumbs. Add vanilla extract. Stir in ¼ cup boiling water until the mixture is evenly moistened. Set aside.

3. In a separate bowl, dissolve the cornstarch in ¼ cup cold water. Mix in the remaining ½ cup white sugar, remaining 1 teaspoon cinnamon, turbinado sugar, lemon juice, and blackberries. Toss the blackberries evenly. Transfer mixture to a skillet and bring to a boil, stirring frequently.

4. Pour blackberry mixture into the baking pan. Drop dough over the mixture by spoonfuls.

5. Bake in preheated oven for 30 minutes, or until topping is golden brown.

HARVEST APPLES PIE

Though trespassing in the woods is illegal in District 12, various members of the Seam ignore the rules to harvest apples in the fall, an act that falls right in line with the apple's reputation as something sinful, or wrong. But those who toe the line between right and wrong successfully could make this delicious fresh apple pie.
(*The Hunger Games*, Chapter 1)

Yields 1 pie, or 6–8 servings

Dough for 9" double-crust pie

¾ cup (1 ½ sticks) unsalted butter

3 tablespoons all-purpose flour

1/3 cup water

½ cup white sugar

½ cup brown sugar

1 teaspoon vanilla extract

2 teaspoons ground cinnamon

½ teaspoon nutmeg

6 Granny Smith apples, peeled, cored, and sliced

½ cup granulated sugar

1 teaspoon cinnamon

¼ cup milk

1. Preheat oven to 350°F.

2. In a large saucepan, melt butter. Stir in the flour to form a paste. Add water, white sugar, and brown sugar. Bring to a boil, reduce temperature, and let syrup simmer for around five minutes. Add vanilla, cinnamon, and nutmeg.

3. Roll out one pie crust and place in a 9" pie pan.

4. Place sliced apples in a large bowl. Mix ¾ of the syrup mixture with the apples, then pile apple mixture into pie crust. Cover with lattice crust, and then pour rest of syrup on top. Be careful not to allow syrup to run off of pie.

5. Bake in preheated oven for 45–60 minutes, until apples are soft.

6. Ten minutes before end of minimum baking time, mix granulated sugar and cinnamon together. Brush top of pie with milk and sprinkle with cinnamon-sugar mixture.

7. Serve pie warm, by itself or with vanilla ice cream.

Tips from Your Sponsor

When you pour the syrup on top of the pie crust, make sure the syrup is still hot. Otherwise it will thicken and prove unwieldy. Prior to piling in the apple mixture, try brushing egg whites over the bottom crust to prevent sogginess.

While it might sound scary, a lattice crust is actually quite easy to do! Just follow these simple instructions:

After you've rolled out half of your dough and lined your pie dish with it (being careful to make sure the dough extends beyond the rim of the dish by at least half an inch), put it in the refrigerator to chill so you can concentrate on the lattice crust.

On a lightly floured surface, roll out the other half of your pie dough. It should roll out to roughly the same extent as the first half of the dough. If this dough feels too soft, try rolling it out on a cookie sheet and letting it chill in your fridge for about half an hour.

Cut the dough into even strips, about ½" wide. After you have filled your pie with its filling, lay out 5–8 parallel strips of the pie dough, depending on how thick your strips are, on top of the filling, with about ½"–¾" space between them. Fold back halfway every other strip.

Place one long strip of dough perpendicular to the parallel strips. Unfold the folded strips over the perpendicular strip. Then take the parallel strips that are running underneath the perpendicular strip and fold them back over the perpendicular strip. Lay down a second perpendicular strip of dough next to the first strip, with about the same space between the strips. Unfold the folded parallel strips over the second strip.

Continue this process until the weave is complete. Trim the edges of the strips flush with the dough of the underlying pie dish, which should be about half an inch over the sides. Fold back the rim of the shell over the edge of the lattice strips, and crimp to secure.

HARVEST HEIRLOOM APPLE CAKE

Here is another dessert easily made with the apples harvested from the restricted forest. This versatile cake is made with simple ingredients that are likely accessible (maybe with a little haggling) to any citizen of District 12.
(*The Hunger Games*, Chapter 1)

Yields 8–10 servings

3 cups all-purpose flour

2 cups sugar

1 teaspoon baking soda

1 teaspoon pumpkin pie spice

2 teaspoons cinnamon

1 teaspoon sea salt

1¼ cups vegetable oil

3 eggs, beaten

2 teaspoons vanilla extract

6 heirloom apples, peeled, cored, and chopped

1 cup walnuts, chopped

Tips from Your Sponsor

If no heirloom apples are available, try using Jonathan, Red Delicious, or Golden Delicious apples.

1. Preheat oven to 375°F. Lightly grease a 9" springform pan.

2. Combine flour, sugar, baking soda, pumpkin pie spice, cinnamon, and salt. Stir to blend. Stir in oil, eggs, and vanilla extract. The mixture will be dense.

3. Stir in apples and nuts. Pour batter into springform pan and bake for about 75 minutes or until the top of the cake is crusty and dark brown.

4. Remove from oven and let cool for 15–20 minutes. Run a knife around the edges of the cake before releasing it from the springform pan. Will keep for several days at room temperature.

SAUTÉED APPLES WITH
AMBER HONEY WHIPPED CREAM

This sweet and savory apple dessert, with its easily acquired ingredients, would likely be the most desired dessert in the Seam simply due to its familiarity via the accessibility of its ingredients. (*The Hunger Games*, Chapter 1)

Yields 6–8 servings

1 cup heavy cream

¾ cup sour cream

¼ cup amber-colored honey

6 tablespoons unsalted butter

6 tart apples, peeled, cored, and sliced

2/3 cup golden raisins

½ cup dried apples, roughly chopped

½ cup light brown sugar

1 teaspoon lemon zest

1 teaspoon ground cinnamon

¼ teaspoon nutmeg

Tips from Your Sponsor

When whipping your own cream, don't expect to reach the stiffness acquired in pre-packaged spray cans of whipped cream. In fact, if you overwhip the cream, you'll turn it into butter. Save overwhipped cream by adding something like sour cream or yogurt or any liquid.

1. In a small bowl, whip the cream and fold in the sour cream and honey. Set aside.

2. Melt the butter in a large skillet and add the remaining ingredients. Sauté for about 10–15 minutes or until apples have softened but are not mushy.

3. Divide apples into pretty bowls and spoon the honeyed whipped cream over the top.

BAKERS' SECRET BANANA BREAD

While the French Bread from the Mellark Family Bakery (Chapter 2) is delicious, it's likely that fine yeast breads aren't the bakery's only bread offerings. This moist and undeniably sweet banana bread works for a morning munch or nighttime dessert.
(*The Hunger Games*, Chapter 1)

Yields 1 8" x 8" pan (or 4" x 8" loaf pan), or 8–10 servings

4 ripe bananas, mashed

½ cup (1 stick) melted butter

¾ cup white sugar

¼ cup turbinado sugar

1 egg, beaten

2 teaspoons vanilla extract

1 teaspoon baking soda

Pinch of kosher salt

1½ cups all-purpose flour

Tips from Your Sponsor

Don't have turbinado sugar on hand? Feel free to replace with regular white sugar. For even more sweetness, try adding 1–2 cups semisweet chocolate chips to this recipe (though the bread will take about ten to fifteen minutes longer to bake). For a less-sweet bread, reduce total amount of sugar to ½ cup.

1. Preheat oven to 350°F. Oil one 8" x 8" pan or one 4" x 8" loaf pan.

2. In a large bowl, mix together mashed bananas and butter. Add both sugars, egg, and vanilla extract. Once thoroughly combined, mix in baking soda and salt. Finally, add flour. Mix well to combine.

3. Pour mixture into prepared pan. Bake for 45–60 minutes, or until toothpick inserted in center comes out clean. Cool on rack. Remove bread from pan and serve.

SWEET POTATO CASSEROLE

Sweet potatoes, like the Katniss tubers for which Katniss is named, are an important root vegetable. The brown sugar and allspice in this recipe give the humble sweet potato a sweet, almost celebratory taste, which those in Capitol—if not Katniss—may associate with the Hunger Games.
(*The Hunger Games,* Chapter 3)

Yields 1 9" x 13" pan, or 8–10 servings

6 large sweet potatoes

½ cup packed brown sugar

½ cup white sugar

2 eggs, beaten

1 teaspoon kosher salt

1 cup (2 sticks) butter, softened

¼ cup whole milk

1 teaspoon vanilla extract

Tips from Your Sponsor

For added sweetness, try a simple crumb topping: Combine ½ cup brown sugar and ⅓ cup all-purpose flour. Mix in 3 tablespoons softened butter until the mixture is coarse, like bread crumbs. Mix in ½ cup pecans and sprinkle the entire mixture on top of the casserole before baking.

1. Preheat oven to 350°F. Lightly grease a 9" x 13" baking dish.

2. Using a fork, poke 8–10 deep holes into each potato. Bake potatoes for 1 hour or until tender. Remove potatoes from oven, and lower the oven temperature to 325°F.

3. Scoop out sweet potato flesh and mash in a large bowl. While potatoes are still hot, mix in brown sugar, white sugar, eggs, salt, butter, milk, and vanilla extract. Mix until smooth. Transfer to baking dish.

4. Bake in the preheated oven for 45 minutes or until lightly browned.

BUTTER COOKIES FROM PEETA'S FATHER

When Peeta's father gave cookies to Katniss before she left for the Capitol, she quickly threw them out the train window. Here the cookies represent Katniss's rejection of a friendship with her fellow tribute. She wants to come home alive, not grow emotionally attached to someone whom she'll have to kill or who will kill her later on in the game. It's too bad; she would have loved these delicious Butter Cookies. (*The Hunger Games*, Chapter 4)

Yields 1 dozen cookies

1 cup (2 sticks) unsalted butter

1 cup granulated sugar, plus more for kneading dough

½ teaspoon salt

2 teaspoons pure vanilla extract

1 large egg yolk

2 cups all-purpose flour

Tips from Your Sponsor

Try mixing ½ cup of cocoa powder with the flour for a chocolate butter cookie. Want to turn these cookies into shapes? Roll out chilled log with a rolling pin until dough reaches desired thickness, then cut into shapes freehand or using cookie cutters. Place lemon curd on top of cooled cookies for an extra-special treat.

1. In a bowl, beat butter, sugar, salt, and vanilla together until smooth and creamy.

2. Add egg yolk; beat until fully incorporated.

3. Add flour 1 cup at a time, beating until just barely mixed.

4. Sprinkle sugar on a clean surface. Place dough on top and knead until the dough smoothes out.

5. Roll dough into one long log about 1½" in diameter. Cover log securely with plastic wrap. Chill dough for at least 2 hours.

6. Preheat oven to 325°F. Oil one large baking sheet.

7. Unwrap chilled log. Slice dough into 1/8"-thick cookies and place about an inch apart on prepared baking sheet. Make sure cookies are still cold when placed in oven to avoid spreading.

8. Bake until the cookies just begin to turn golden around the edges, about 15–18 minutes. Serve with a cold glass of milk.

BROWN SUGAR SHORTBREAD

When Mr. Mellark gave Katniss the butter cookies, he wasn't thinking clearly. After all, cookies that are thick and fairly sturdy, such as this shortbread, travel much better than their thinner counterparts. If you're sending these cookies on a trip of some kind, make sure to pack them fairly tightly—loosely packed cookies will move around and have a greater chance of breaking.
(*The Hunger Games*, Chapter 3)

Makes 24 squares

½ cup unsalted butter, softened

2 cups dark brown sugar, firmly packed

3 eggs

1 ½ cups all-purpose flour

1 teaspoon baking powder

¼ teaspoon kosher salt

2 teaspoons vanilla extract

Tips from Your Sponsor

Not a fan of dark brown sugar? Try this recipe with light brown sugar for a more buttery and less molasses-flavored cookie.

1. Preheat the oven to 350°F. Lightly grease a 9" x 13" baking pan and set aside.

2. Cream butter and sugar together in a large bowl until fully combined, at least 5 minutes. Add eggs one at a time and continue to mix until light and fluffy.

3. Sift flour, baking powder, and salt together. Add to the creamed mixture and combine until smooth. Add the vanilla and mix once more.

4. Pour batter into prepared pan and spread evenly. Bake in preheated oven for 30 minutes, or until golden brown.

5. Let shortbread cool for at least 15 minutes, then cut into squares.

WHITE CHOCOLATE CHOCOLATE COOKIES

A twist on the classic chocolate chip cookie, this cookie is similar to Katniss's spirit — mostly dark, with patches of light throughout.
(*The Hunger Games*, Chapter 3)

Yields 36 cookies

1 cup (2 sticks) unsalted butter

1 cup white sugar

1 cup brown sugar

2 teaspoons vanilla

Pinch of salt

2 eggs

1¼ cups high-quality unsweetened cocoa powder

1¾ cups all-purpose flour

1 teaspoon baking soda

1 teaspoon baking powder

2 cups high-quality white chocolate chips (such as Guittard)

Tips from Your Sponsor

It's hard to tell when a chocolate cookie is done because it never looks burned. However, if in doubt, it's better to be risky and remove when underbaked rather when overbaked. There's no recovering from a burned cookie!

1. Preheat oven to 350°F. Grease cookie sheets.

2. In a large bowl, cream together the butter, both sugars, vanilla, and salt until light and fluffy. Add the eggs one at a time, beating well after each addition. In a separate bowl, combine the cocoa, flour, baking soda, and baking powder.

3. Gradually stir the flour mixture into the creamed mixture. Fold in the white chocolate chips. Drop dough by rounded spoonfuls onto the prepared cookie sheets.

4. Bake cookies for 8–10 minutes in preheated oven, until puffy but still soft. Allow cookies to cool on baking sheet for 5 minutes before removing to wire racks to cool completely.

SWEET SUGAR COOKIES FROM A SWEETIE

This recipe gives another option for the cookies that Peeta's father gives to Katniss.
(*The Hunger Games*, Chapter 3)

Yields 1 dozen cookies

2¾ cups all-purpose flour

1 teaspoon baking soda

½ teaspoon baking powder

1 teaspoon coarse sea salt

1 egg

1 teaspoon vanilla extract

1 cup (2 sticks) butter, softened

1 cup white sugar

½ cup turbinado sugar

3 tablespoons white sugar

Tips from Your Sponsor

Having a hard time getting the sugar to stick to the balls of dough? Try this trick from *Cook's Illustrated*: Moisten your hands with water, and using your wet hands, form the balls of dough. Then roll the moist balls in the sugar. Whenever your hands lose moisture, rewet. This will help keep the sugar on the dough.

1. In a medium-sized bowl, sift together the flour, baking soda, baking powder, and sea salt. In a small bowl, beat together the egg and vanilla.

2. In a large bowl, cream together the butter, 1 cup white sugar, and the turbinado sugar. Cream until light and fluffy, at least 5 minutes. Add egg and vanilla mixture, mixing completely. Gradually blend in the dry ingredients.

3. Chill dough in the fridge for at least 1 hour. Fifteen minutes before baking, preheat oven to 375°F.

4. Pour 3 tablespoons of white sugar into a small bowl. Roll rounded teaspoonfuls of dough into small balls. Roll balls in sugar, then place onto ungreased cookie sheets.

5. Bake for 8–10 minutes, or until just barely golden brown at the edges. If the cookies don't look completely done, that's okay. Let cookies stand on sheet for 5 minutes before removing to cool on wire rack.

CAPITOL-GRADE DARK CHOCOLATE CAKE

The feast served during Katniss's first night away from her family ends with a decadent chocolate cake. Amidst the depression of facing almost-certain death (not to mention Haymitch's dispiriting drunkenness!), this sweet ending perhaps makes Katniss realize that things aren't as bad as they may seem.
(*The Hunger Games*, Chapter 3)

Yields 1 cake, or 8–10 servings

> Cake:

2 cups all-purpose flour

2 cups white sugar

1 cup fine-quality unsweetened cocoa powder, such as Scharffen Berger

2 teaspoons baking soda

1 teaspoon baking powder

½ teaspoon salt

2 eggs

1 cup cold brewed coffee

1 cup buttermilk

½ cup vegetable oil

> Icing:

2 cups (1 pound) butter (no substitutes), softened

9 cups confectioners' sugar

2½ cups fine-quality unsweetened cocoa powder

1 teaspoon vanilla extract

1 cup milk

1. Preheat oven to 350°F. Grease and flour a 9" x13" pan.

2. In a large bowl, sift together the flour, sugar, cocoa, baking soda, baking powder, and salt. Make a well in the center and pour in the eggs, coffee, buttermilk, and oil. Mix with a wooden spoon until smooth; batter will be thin. Pour into prepared pan.

3. Bake for 35–40 minutes, or until a toothpick inserted into the center of the cake comes out clean. Allow to cool in the pan for 45 minutes.

4. While cake cools, prepare the icing. In a stand mixer with a paddle attachment on medium speed or using a wooden spoon and lots of muscle, beat butter until smooth and creamy. Reduce speed to low and add confectioners' sugar, cocoa, and vanilla, scraping down sides of the bowl with a spatula as you go. Add milk as needed until frosting reaches preferred spreading consistency. (For thicker frosting, add less than a cup of milk. To thin out your frosting, add more milk. The choice is yours!)

5. Once cake has thoroughly cooled, spread icing over the top.

Tips from Your Sponsor

Ever wonder what makes your kitchen smell so good when you're baking a chocolate dessert? When chocolate is heated, its liquids turn to steam and carry away the chemical compounds that make up the chocolate! This allows us cooks a chance to smell the chocolate deliciousness and salivate with anticipation. The bad news? Those yummy chemical compounds are no longer in the chocolate—which is where you want them to be. Yikes! So it's always better to *undercook* rather than *overcook* your chocolate desserts . . . that way you can keep as much chocolate flavor as possible!

BIG SOFTIE GINGER COOKIES

All bakers must possess three definitive cookies in their repertoire: a chocolate chip cookie recipe, a sugar cookie recipe, and last but certainly not least, a ginger cookie recipe. This is a cookie that is as soft and gooey as Peeta's affection for Katniss, and is likely one Katniss has smelled during her many walks by the bakery.
(*The Hunger Games*, Chapter 4)

Yields 2 dozen cookies

2½ cups all-purpose flour

2 teaspoons ground ginger

1 teaspoon baking soda

2 teaspoons ground cinnamon

1 teaspoon ground cloves

1 teaspoon kosher salt

1 cup (2 sticks) butter, softened

½ cup white sugar

½ cup light brown sugar

1 egg

1 teaspoon vanilla extract

1 tablespoon orange juice

¼ cup molasses

4 tablespoons white sugar

Tips from Your Sponsor

There's a reason for every step in this recipe! The tablespoon of orange juice helps bring out the ginger flavor. Meanwhile, because the molasses tends to make the dough sticky, refrigerating the dough makes it easier to shape into balls before rolling in sugar and baking.

1. Preheat oven to 350°F.

2. In a large bowl, sift together the flour, ginger, baking soda, cinnamon, cloves, and salt.

3. In a separate large bowl, cream together the butter, ½ cup white sugar, and the brown sugar until light and fluffy. Beat in the egg and vanilla, then stir in the orange juice and molasses. Gradually stir the sifted ingredients into the molasses mixture. Chill dough for 1 hour in refrigerator.

4. Place the 4 tablespoons white sugar in a small bowl. Shape chilled dough into gumball-sized balls, and roll them in the sugar. Place the cookies 2 inches apart onto an ungreased cookie sheet.

5. Bake for 8–10 minutes in the preheated oven. Allow cookies to cool on baking sheet for 5 minutes before removing to a wire rack to cool completely.

PUFFY WHITE CHOCOLATE-
BLUEBERRY MUFFIN TOPS

A unique cookie—the juxtaposition of sweet white chocolate with tart blueberries within each bite would get any baker noticed and praised. With the amount of wild blueberries likely growing out and about the Seam (not to mention Katniss's willingness to sell Mr. Mellark any of the wild berries she finds), this is sure to be a successful dessert enjoyed by the poor and rich alike of District 12. (*The Hunger Games,* Chapter 4)

Yields 1 dozen cookies

2½ cups all-purpose flour

1 teaspoon baking powder

¼ plus 1/8 teaspoon baking soda

1 teaspoon kosher salt

1 cup (2 sticks) butter, softened

½ cup white sugar

½ cup packed light brown sugar

3 eggs

2 teaspoons vanilla extract

1 cup white chocolate chips (preferably high-quality such as Guittard)

1 cup fresh blueberries

Tips from Your Sponsor

These muffin tops are really just very cakelike cookies. These delicious and incredibly soft cookies will be ready when their edges turn brown. Keep in mind that the longer they bake, the less cakelike they will be.

1. Preheat oven to 400°F. Grease cookie sheets.

2. In a medium-sized bowl, sift together the flour, baking powder, baking soda, and salt. Set aside.

3. Cream the butter with the sugars until light and fluffy. Beat in the eggs and vanilla. Add the flour mixture, and stir until just combined. Stir in the white chocolate chips and blueberries.

4. Drop dough by spoonfuls onto prepared cookie sheets. Don't worry, they won't spread too far.

5. Bake in preheated oven for 12–15 minutes. Remove from oven, and let cool on cookie sheet for five minutes before placing on cooling racks.

STRAWBERRY SHORTBREAD BARS

Mayor Undersee has a fondness for strawberries, so this strawberry shortbread is sure to be a hit in the mayor's house. It's likely to be enjoyed by both the mayor and his daughter, Madge.
(*The Hunger Games*, Chapter 4)

Yields 1 dozen bars

1¼ pounds (5 sticks) unsalted butter, slightly softened

5 egg yolks

2 teaspoons vanilla extract

2½ cups granulated sugar

4½ cups all-purpose flour

2 teaspoons baking powder

½ teaspoon salt

3 cups strawberry jam, room temperature

1 cup fresh strawberries, chopped

½ cup confectioners' sugar

Tips from Your Sponsor

If strawberries are not your favorite fruit, you can use this same recipe for a different berry shortbread, such as blueberry shortbread. Instead of strawberry jam, use blueberry jam, and fresh blueberries instead of fresh strawberries!

1. Cream the butter until soft and fluffy. Add egg yolks and vanilla; mix well.

2. In a large bowl, combine the granulated sugar, flour, baking powder, and salt. Mix in the butter and egg mixture until just barely incorporated.

3. Turn the dough out onto a well-floured surface and form into two balls. Wrap each ball tightly in plastic wrap and freeze at least 2 hours.

4. Preheat oven to 350°F.

5. Remove one ball of dough from the freezer and coarsely grate it by hand onto the bottom of a 9" x 13" baking pan. Make sure to evenly coat the surface with shreds of dough.

6. Spread jam evenly over the dough surface. Evenly distribute fresh strawberries over jam. Remove the remaining dough from the freezer and coarsely grate over the strawberry filling, sandwiching it.

7. Bake in preheated oven until lightly golden brown and center no longer wiggles, about 1 hour. Dust the confectioners' sugar over the top of the shortbread as soon as it's removed from the oven.

8. Cool, then let chill in fridge for at least 1 hour. Cut bars out of pan with serrated knife. Serve.

OPPORTUNISTIC STRAWBERRY BREAD

It's likely that Katniss isn't the only one aware of the mayor's penchant for strawberries. In fact, Peeta's father, perhaps recognizing an opportunity to support his family, probably makes this yummy strawberry bread specifically to sell to the mayor!
(*The Hunger Games*, Chapter 4)

Makes 1 loaf

¼ cup honey

¼ cup (½ stick) butter, melted

1 egg, beaten

1½ cups whole wheat flour

3 teaspoons baking powder

1 cup strawberries

Tips from Your Sponsor

For an especially lovely (not to mention tasty) presentation, sprinkle ½ cup of confectioners' sugar over the loaf once it's removed from the pan. Or, for an especially sweet snack, try spreading cream cheese and strawberry preserves across the top.

1. Preheat oven to 325°F. Grease a 9" loaf pan.

2. Add honey and butter to beaten egg and blend.

3. Put flour and baking powder in a large bowl and make a well in the center.

4. Pour in egg mixture and add strawberries. Blend well.

5. Pour into greased loaf pan and bake about 1 hour. Bread is done when toothpick inserted in center comes out clean.

6. Cool 10–15 minutes before removing from pan.

PEETA'S SPIRIT-LIFTING HOT CHOCOLATE WITH VANILLA WHIPPED CREAM

Drinking the Capitol's hot chocolate is one of the few enjoyable parts of being involved in the spectacle that surrounds the Hunger Games. Both Peeta and Katniss would love this decadent, delicious recipe.
(*The Hunger Games*, Chapter 4)

Yields 4 servings

> Cocoa:

1/3 cup unsweetened cocoa powder

½ cup white sugar

½ teaspoon salt

1/3 cup boiling water

3½ cups milk

2 teaspoons high-quality vanilla extract

½ cup half-and-half

Handful of semisweet chocolate chips

> Whipped Cream:

1 cup heavy cream

2 teaspoons vanilla extract

½ cup confectioners' sugar

Tips from Your Sponsor

Want to give this sweet hot chocolate a bit of a kick? Add 1 teaspoon cinnamon and ¼ teaspoon cayenne pepper to the cocoa powder. Often called Mayan Hot Chocolate, this form of hot chocolate remains sweet and addictive, with just enough spice. Ground ginger is a fun addition, as well.

1. Place a medium-sized metal bowl in the freezer to chill.

2. Combine the cocoa, sugar, and salt in a saucepan. Stir in boiling water and keep stirring as you bring the mixture to a boil. Simmer and stir for 3 minutes, being careful not to let the mixture scorch. Add milk, half and half, and chocolate chips over high heat, but do not boil. Remove from heat once chocolate chips have thoroughly melted and add vanilla. Divide among 4 mugs.

3. Whip heavy cream in the chilled metal bowl until soft peaks are just about to form. Add vanilla and confectioners' sugar and continue beating until the cream holds it shape. Do not overbeat. Dollop onto hot chocolate in mugs.

HEART OF ICE FROZEN HOT CHOCOLATE

While Katniss and Peeta normally enjoy hot chocolate, this frozen version is a worthy substitute for hot cocoa on a warm, sunny day.
(*The Hunger Games,* Chapter 4)

Yields 1 serving

6 ounces high-quality semisweet chocolate

1 teaspoon vanilla extract

3 teaspoons high-quality hot chocolate mix

2 tablespoons sugar

1½ cups half and half

2 cups ice

Whipped cream (for garnish)

Chocolate shavings (for garnish)

Tips from Your Sponsor

For a mint-chocolate taste, try adding ½ teaspoon of mint extract. Or, for a sweeter taste, mix together 3 ounces white chocolate and 3 ounces semisweet chocolate in place of the 6 ounces semisweet.

1. Chop the chocolate into small pieces and gently melt in a heavy saucepan, stirring constantly until completely melted. Add the vanilla extract, hot chocolate mix, and sugar, stirring thoroughly until well-blended.

2. Remove from heat and slowly add ½ cup of the half and half, stirring until smooth. Let cool to room temperature.

3. Place ice, remaining 1 cup of half and half, and chocolate mixture into a blender. Blend until the mixture reaches a smoothie-like consistency. Pour into a large cup and top with whipped cream and chocolate shavings.

HONEY CARAMEL CUSTARD FOR YOUR HONEY

Katniss is so unused to sweets that she can't even guess what ingredients are in this beautiful honey-colored pudding that she sits down to eat with Cinna. Nonetheless, the sugary honey is likely a physical indicator of the sweet relationship that will soon develop between Katniss and her stylist. (*The Hunger Games*, Chapter 5)

Yields 4 servings

2 cups whipping cream

2 teaspoons honey

4 egg yolks

2 teaspoons vanilla extract

¼ cup sugar

1 teaspoon honey

¼ teaspoon salt

3 cups very hot water

½–1 cup brown sugar

Tips from Your Sponsor

Not all custards are sweet! To be considered a custard, the dish must be an egg-thickened custard. This means the often-savory quiche is also technically a custard. If gelatin is used as the thickening agent instead of egg, the dish is known as crème anglaise collée.

1. Mix whipping cream and 2 teaspoons honey in a small saucepan. Place saucepan over medium-low heat and bring cream mixture almost to a simmer.

2. Preheat oven to 350°F.

3. In a mixing bowl, beat egg yolks, vanilla, sugar, honey, and salt until thick, about 3 minutes. Gradually beat in cream mixture. Pour into an ungreased 8" X 8" broiler-proof baking dish. Let sit for 5 minutes.

4. Place baking dish into a 13" x 9" x 2" baking pan. Pour the hot water into baking pan to a depth of at least 1 inch. Bake in preheated oven for 60 minutes or until a knife inserted near the center of the custard comes out clean.

5. Remove custard from the hot water and cool on a wire rack for 30 minutes. Refrigerate until chilled, at least 2 hours.

6. Thirty minutes before serving, remove custard from refrigerator. Preheat broiler. Sprinkle top of custard with brown sugar. Broil the custard 6 inches from the heat for 2 minutes or until brown sugar is melted. Remove from oven.

7. Chill for another 30 minutes before serving.

SPIRITED CHOCOLATE FUDGE CAKE WITH CHOCOLATE PUDDING FROSTING

The cakes Katniss sees in the Capitol are all unbelievably decadent. This cake evokes the rich, extravagent feeling many in the Capitol experience daily. The orange juice in the frosting and the coffee granules in the cake give this dessert a special kick.
(*The Hunger Games*, Chapter 6)

Yields 1 cake, or 8–10 servings

> Cake:

Nonstick vegetable oil cooking spray

2 cups sifted cake flour

2 tablespoons instant coffee granules

1 cup high-quality unsweetened cocoa powder

1¼ teaspoons baking soda

½ teaspoon baking powder

1 teaspoon kosher salt

2 cups packed golden brown sugar

2 cups (1 pound) unsalted butter, room temperature

3 large eggs

2 tablespoons vanilla extract

1 cup plus 2 tablespoons buttermilk

½ cup lukewarm water

1½ cups semisweet chocolate chips

> Frosting:

1½ cups sugar

3½ tablespoons cornstarch

½ teaspoon salt

4 ounces unsweetened chocolate, finely chopped

1 milk

1 tablespoon orange juice

4 tablespoons (½ stick) unsalted butter, softened and cut into pieces

Tips from Your Sponsor

For a smooth cake, let it sit for an hour after frosting between the layers and before frosting the outside of the cake. Then, using a small amount of frosting, coat the sides of the cake, and then the top. This first thin coating on the outside will form a base for the final frosting. Expect to frost a few inches at a time, and do not lift the spatula from the cake until you finish one small, clean swipe. After completing the first layer of frosting on the outside of cake, refrigerate for 20 minutes . . . and then frost again.

1. Preheat oven to 350°F. Spray three 9" cake plans with nonstick cooking spray. Line bottoms of pans with parchment paper. Using the pans as a template, cut out three 9" diameter rounds from cardboard; set aside.

2. In a medium-size bowl, whisk together flour, coffee granules, cocoa powder, baking soda, baking powder, and salt. Set aside.

3. Using an electric mixer, beat brown sugar and butter in a large bowl until fluffy, about 2–3 minutes. Add eggs one at a time, beating well after each addition. Beat in vanilla.

4. Slowly beat in dry ingredients and buttermilk in alternating small portions, starting and ending with the dry ingredients. Beat in ½ cup lukewarm water. Stir in chocolate chips.

5. Divide batter among prepared pans, about 2½ cups for each. Smooth tops. Bake cake layers until toothpick inserted into center comes out clean, about 25 minutes.

6. Cool cake layers completely in pans on racks. When cool, invert each layer onto a 9" cardboard round. Warning—cakes are delicate. Peel off parchment.

7. For the frosting: In a heavy saucepan whisk together the sugar, cornstarch, salt, and the chocolate. Add the milk. Bring the mixture to a boil over medium heat, whisking constantly. Simmer, still whisking, for 2–3 minutes. Add the orange juice.

8. Transfer the mixture to a small metal bowl. Using an electric mixer, beat in the butter until it's completely incorporated. Set the bowl in a larger bowl filled with ice and cold water and continue beating the frosting until it is light and holds soft peaks.

9. To assemble the cake: On a cake stand arrange 1 cake layer, spread the top with some of the frosting, and top with the second cake layer. Spread the second layer with more frosting and top that with the final cake layer. Spread the sides and top of the cake with the remaining frosting.

PEETA'S BUTTERCREAM FROSTING

Peeta is quite skilled when it comes to frosting and decorating his family's bakery cakes. This buttercream frosting can be used for cakes, cupcakes, or any dessert concoction, and is likely used by Peeta for many of the desserts that Prim and Katniss admired in the bakery window.
(*The Hunger Games*, Chapter 7)

Yields about 8 cups

1½ cups shortening

½ cup (1 stick) butter

8 cups confectioners' sugar

1 teaspoon salt

3 teaspoons clear imitation vanilla extract

¾ cup heavy cream

Tips from Your Sponsor

The flavor of clear imitation vanilla extract pales in comparison to natural vanilla extract. However, for a white frosting, clear imitation vanilla extract is a must, as real vanilla extract is a light brown color.

1. Using an electric mixer, cream shortening and butter together until light and very, very fluffy, at least 8 minutes. Add confectioners' sugar and continue creaming until extremely well blended.

2. Slowly add salt, vanilla, and heavy cream on a low speed until moistened. Then beat at high speed until the frosting is once again fluffy.

Thick, juicy plums were one of the treats Gale and Katniss were able to find during their forays into the wild. This plum cake would be a scrumptious use of those found plums.
(*The Hunger Games*, Chapter 8)

Yields 8–10 servings

½ cup (1 stick) unsalted butter, softened

1½ cups sugar

¼ cup heavy cream

2 teaspoons vanilla extract

Zest of 1 lemon

3 large eggs

1½ cups all-purpose flour

1 teaspoon baking powder

¼ teaspoon kosher salt

2 pounds plums

3 teaspoons cinnamon

Tips from Your Sponsor

This cake is delicious on its own or with a scoop of French vanilla ice cream! Either way, be sure to use red or purple plums in this recipe, as smallish yellow plums, sometimes referred to as sand plums, are very hard and bitter and best used for jams and jellies.

1. Preheat the oven to 350°F. Butter and flour a 9" springform pan and set aside.

2. Cream the butter and 1 cup of the sugar. Add the heavy cream, vanilla, and lemon zest. Add eggs one at a time, blending well after each.

3. Mix the flour, baking powder, and salt together. Add to the batter and combine until just blended. Pour into the prepared springform pan.

4. Pit and slice the plums and toss with the remaining ½ cup sugar and 2 teaspoons of the ground cinnamon.

5. Lay slices of plums, all in the same direction and slightly overlapping, along the outside edge of the pan. Then, positioning the plum slices the opposite way, layer inward in a concentric circle. Repeat again with another smaller circle going in the opposite direction, reserving 2 or 3 slices to mound in the middle for a pretty finish. Sprinkle remaining cinnamon on top of plums.

6. Bake for about 60 minutes or until the cake no longer jiggles when slightly shaken. Let cool. Run a knife around the pan edge. Release the springform and serve cake at room temperature.

THE TASTE OF GALE'S KISS: SWEET ORANGE CAKE

When Gale surprises Katniss with a kiss, she notes that his kiss tastes like oranges, a fruit that often symbolizes happiness and prosperity. While this cake might not pack the romantic punch that Gale's kiss does, it's a sweet surrogate for those of us with no Gale or Peeta in our lives. (*Catching Fire*, Chapter 2)

Yields one 2-layer cake, or 8–10 servings

> Crunch Layer:

2 cups graham cracker crumbs

¾ cup brown sugar

½ cup sliced almonds

1 cup (2 sticks) butter, softened

1 teaspoon vanilla extract

> Cake:

1 package yellow cake mix

½ cup water

½ cup fresh-squeezed orange juice

1/3 cup vegetable oil

3 eggs

1 teaspoon orange extract

> Frosting:

1 cup (2 sticks) unsalted butter, softened

2 8-ounce packages cream cheese, softened

1 tablespoon plus 1 teaspoon vanilla extract

4 cups sifted confectioners' sugar

1 tablespoon plus 1 teaspoon fresh-squeezed orange juice

½ cup whole milk (optional)

1. Preheat oven to 350°F. Oil and flour two 9" pans.

2. For the crunch layer: In a small bowl, mix together the graham cracker crumbs, brown sugar, almonds, butter, and vanilla extract. Divide the mixture evenly between the two prepared pans. Set aside.

3. For cake: Combine the cake mix, water, orange juice, and oil until just blended. Beat in the eggs one at a time, then stir in orange extract. Stir until thoroughly combined. Pour the mixture evenly over the crunch layer in the pans.

4. Bake the cakes in the preheated oven for 30–35 minutes, or until a toothpick inserted comes out clean. Remove pans from oven and allow to cool for at least 15 minutes. Invert pans onto a wire rack and let cakes cool completely before frosting.

5. For frosting: In a medium-sized bowl, beat together the butter, cream cheese, vanilla extract, sugar, and orange juice. If too thick, add up to ½ cup whole milk.

6. Once cakes are thoroughly cooled, frost crunch-side-up. Layer cakes on top of one another, and thoroughly frost top and sides.

Tips from Your Sponsor

As an added touch of class, try placing some mandarin orange slices or curled orange skins on top of the cake for an extra-tasty garnish!

PARCEL DAY APPLESAUCE

This applesauce is both sweet and filling, a perfect treat for the children of the Seam on Parcel Day. (*Catching Fire*, Chapter 2)

Yields 4 servings

6 apples, peeled, cored, and chopped

¾ cup water

½ cup white sugar

1 teaspoon ground cinnamon

Tips from Your Sponsor

Different types of apples vary in sweetness. Macintosh and Empire apples, for instance, are sweeter than other kinds, so your applesauce might call for less sugar depending on your taste. Experiment with different varieties of apples to come up with your own personal-favorite applesauce.

1. In a large saucepan, combine apples, water, sugar, and cinnamon. Cover and cook over medium heat for 30 minutes, or until apples are soft.

2. Allow to cool, then mash with a fork or potato masher.

BOISTEROUS BLUEBERRY MUFFINS FOR HAYMITCH

Haymitch picks at a muffin when he meets Katniss and Peeta for lunch on the train ride tour to the Capitol, illustrating just how depleted he has become by the Victory Tour: He's so affected he can't even manage to eat a small meal. Despite his less-than-enthusiastic response, you'll love this delicious recipe. (*Catching Fire*, Chapter 4)

Yields 10 large muffins

> Crumb Topping:

½ cup brown sugar

1/3 cup all-purpose flour

½ cup (1 stick) butter, cubed and room temperature

2 teaspoons cinnamon

> Muffins:

1½ cups all-purpose flour

½ cup white sugar

½ cup turbinado sugar

½ teaspoon kosher salt

2 teaspoons baking powder

1/3 cup vegetable oil

1 egg, beaten

1/3 cup buttermilk

1 teaspoon vanilla extract

1½ cups fresh blueberries

1. Preheat oven to 400°F. Grease 10 large muffin cups or line with paper baking cups.

2. Prepare crumb topping: Mix together ½ cup brown sugar, 1/3 cup all-purpose flour, butter cubes, and 2 teaspoons cinnamon. Mix together with fork. Set aside.

3. For muffins: Combine 1½ cups flour, white sugar, turbinado sugar, salt, and baking powder.

4. Pour vegetable oil into a 1-cup measuring cup. Add the egg and enough buttermilk to fill the cup. Mix this and vanilla with flour mixture just until the dry ingredients are moistened. Fold in blueberries, being careful not to stir the mixture too much.

5. Fill muffin cups right to the top. Sprinkle with crumb topping mixture.

6. Bake for 20–25 minutes in the preheated oven, or until toothpick inserted in center of muffin comes out clean.

Tips from Your Sponsor

If you overstir the batter when combining the wet and dry ingredients or when adding the blueberries, the muffins will not rise. Instead, combine ingredients with the fewest strokes possible. The thicker the batter, the better the muffin!

ATTACK OF THE CHOCOLATE CHUNK MUFFINS

These gooey chocolate muffins are made with pure, high-quality semisweet chocolate chunks and milk chocolate chips. As such, they will definitely cure whatever sweet tooth Haymitch may acquire in an attempt to find some pleasantness while guiding Katniss and Peeta safely through the Hunger Games. (*The Hunger Games*, Chapter 4)

Yields 12 muffins

10 ounces high-quality semisweet chocolate chunks

1 ¼ cups all-purpose flour

½ teaspoon baking soda

1 teaspoon baking powder

½ teaspoon salt

½ teaspoon vanilla extract

½ teaspoon almond extract

2/3 cup whole milk

½ cup (1 stick) unsalted butter, softened

1 cup packed light brown sugar

2 large eggs

1 cup high-quality milk chocolate chips

Tips from Your Sponsor

Lacking paper cup liners for your muffins? That's not a problem. Just thoroughly grease your muffin pan and pour the batter directly in, as if it were a cake. After they've thoroughly cooled, carefully tap the pan sideways on the counter . . . the muffins should just fall right out.

1. Preheat oven to 350°F. Line muffin cups with paper baking cups.

2. Melt semisweet chocolate in a metal bowl set over a pan of barely simmering water. (Do not let any of the water get into the chocolate.) Stir constantly while the chocolate melts. Remove bowl from heat and let cool slightly.

3. Whisk together flour, baking soda, baking powder, and salt.

4. In a separate bowl, whisk vanilla and almond extracts into milk.

5. Beat butter with brown sugar in a large bowl until pale and fluffy. This might take a while if doing by hand. Then add eggs 1 at a time, beating well with each addition. Slowly add melted chocolate; beat well. Alternately mix in flour mixture and milk, starting and ending with flour, scraping down sides of bowl after each addition. Fold in milk chocolate chips.

6. Divide batter among lined muffin cups. Bake for 30–35 minutes or until toothpick inserted in the center of a muffin comes out clean. Cool muffins in pans for 10–15 minutes, then invert onto racks to cool.

THICK AND GOOEY DOUBLE CHOCOLATE BANQUET BROWNIES

Brownies are the ultimate dessert finger food. When made correctly, one small brownie can be just as filling as a large piece of cake and infinitely more filling than a cookie. No banquet sweets table is complete without a delicious chocolate brownie.
(*Catching Fire*, Chapter 6)

Yields 24 servings

2 cups (1 pound) unsalted butter

1 (12-ounce) bag semisweet chocolate chips (preferably Guittard)

2 (12-ounce) bags milk chocolate chips (preferably Guittard)

6 large eggs, beaten

2 tablespoons vanilla extract

2½ cups granulated sugar

1½ cups all-purpose flour

1 tablespoon baking powder

1 teaspoon kosher salt

Tips from Your Sponsor

It's not necessary to use a 13" x 9" x 2" pan in this recipe, but keep in mind the smaller your pan, the thicker your brownies, and the longer the required baking time!

1. Preheat oven to 325°F. Grease one 13" x 9" x 2" baking pan.

2. Using a double boiler, melt butter, semisweet chocolate chips, and one bag of the milk chocolate chips. Let this mixture cool slightly but *do not let it harden*. Stir in eggs, vanilla, and sugar.

3. Sift together the flour, baking powder, and salt. Stir flour combination into the chocolate mixture. Mix in the last batch of milk chocolate chips.

4. Spread batter evenly in the prepared pans. Bake for 20–25 minutes. Do not overbake—a toothpick will not come out clean when inserted! Bake just until the center no longer jiggles. As the brownies cool, they will firm up and become like brownie "fudge." Cool completely before cutting and serving.

RED VELVET CAKE WITH CREAM CHEESE FROSTING

Every baker has a red velvet cake recipe in his or her pocket, and it's likely that one of the cakes at the banquet Peeta and Katniss attend before the 75th Hunger Games is red velvet with delicious cream cheese frosting.
(*Catching Fire*, Chapter 6)

Yields 1 cake, 6–8 servings

> Cake:

3 tablespoons unsweetened cocoa powder

2 ounces liquid red food coloring

1 cup buttermilk

1 teaspoon salt

1 teaspoon vanilla extract

1 cup vegetable oil

2 cups white sugar

2 eggs

2½ cups all-purpose flour, sifted

1½ teaspoons baking soda

1 teaspoon white vinegar

> Frosting:

1 (8-ounce) package cream cheese, softened

¾ cup (1½ sticks) unsalted butter, softened

1½ teaspoons vanilla extract

2½ cups sifted confectioners' sugar

1. Preheat oven to 350°F. Grease two 9" round cake pans. Make a paste of the cocoa and food coloring. Set aside.

2. Combine the buttermilk, salt, and 1 teaspoon vanilla. Set aside.

3. In a large bowl, cream together the oil and 1½ cups of the sugar until light and fluffy. Beat in eggs one at a time, then stir in the cocoa mixture. Beat in the buttermilk mixture, alternating with the flour, mixing until just incorporated. Stir together the baking soda and vinegar; gently fold into the cake batter.

4. Pour batter into prepared pans. Bake in the preheated oven for 30 minutes, or until a toothpick inserted in the center comes out clean. Let cake cool in pans for 15 minutes before removing by sliding a butter knife around the edges and turning upside down onto a prepared cutting board, then flipping over. Allow to cool completely before frosting. After frosting, refrigerate until ready to serve.

5. For frosting: In a medium bowl, cream together the cream cheese and butter. Add vanilla, then gradually stir in the confectioners' sugar. For a thinner consistency, add a touch of milk.

Tips from Your Sponsor

Most people would be disgusted to learn that what gives red velvet cake its delicious taste is the white vinegar. Also, if you'd rather not use red food coloring in your cake, try using 9 tablespoons beetroot juice instead.

MILK CHOCOLATE HONEY BROWNIES WITH A KICK

Even the smallest bite of these brownies packs a quiet punch, much like a conversation—or almost any interaction—with Katniss.
(*Catching Fire*, Chapter 6)

Yields 24 servings

1 cup butter

1 12-ounce bag high-quality semisweet chocolate chips

1¼ cups all-purpose flour

1 teaspoon kosher salt

2 cups sugar

2 teaspoons vanilla extract

4 eggs

1 tablespoon honey

Tips from Your Sponsor

Without the honey, this is a pretty standard brownie batter. If you're not a fan of honey, try adding a tablespoon of caramel sauce or dulce de leche. Or sprinkle in a teaspoon of cinnamon and a teaspoon of chipotle powder for some added spice!

1. Preheat oven to 350°F. Grease two 8" x 8" baking pans.

2. In a medium-sized bowl, melt butter and chocolate chips in the microwave for thirty seconds. Remove from microwave, and stir with fork. If not completely melted, heat in microwave (on low if possible) for another thirty seconds. Continue this process until chocolate is thoroughly melted but not burned.

3. In a medium-sized bowl, whisk together flour and salt. Set aside.

4. Stir in sugar, vanilla, and eggs one at a time into the chocolate mixture, followed by honey. Slowly mix in flour mixture. Pour brownie batter into pans.

5. Bake for 40–45 minutes, or until a toothpick inserted into center of brownies comes out clean.

SPICE CAKE WITH HOMEMADE CARAMEL SAUCE

Katniss buys cake from Peeta's father while the Hob burns. It's likely that she would have purchased something warm and comforting, like this spice cake, to take the sting away from her new reality. (*Catching Fire*, Chapter 9)

Yields 10–12 servings

> Spice Cake:

3 cups all-purpose flour

1 tablespoon ground allspice

1 tablespoon ground cinnamon

1 teaspoon baking soda

1/8 teaspoon kosher salt

1 cup (2 sticks) unsalted butter, softened

2 cups white sugar

½ cup light brown sugar

5 eggs

1 cup buttermilk

> Caramel Sauce:

1 cup sugar

¼ cup water

¾ cup heavy cream

Tips from Your Sponsor

The caramel sauce is the real pièce de résistance in this recipe, so don't skip it! For additional flavor, trying adding a half cup of raisins to the cake, tossing them with ¼ of the flour mixture. Sprinkle the coated raisins on top of the batter before baking.

1. Preheat oven to 350°F. Lightly grease a bundt pan and set aside.

2. Sift together flour, spices, baking soda, and salt. Set aside.

3. In a large bowl, cream together the butter and sugars. Add the eggs, one at a time, and beat well.

4. Add the flour mixture alternately with the buttermilk, starting and ending with the flour. Beat only until blended. Pour batter into the prepared bundt pan.

5. Bake for 60–65 minutes or until a toothpick inserted in the middle of the cake comes out clean. Cool on a wire rack for 20 minutes before turning out onto the rack to finish cooling.

6. For caramel sauce: Place 1 cup sugar and ¼ cup water in a heavy saucepan and bring to a boil, stirring frequently. Reduce heat to a simmer and swirl liquid in pan a couple of times (but do not stir) until it's a deep golden brown. Remove from the heat. Slowly whisk in the cream. Let sit for about 5 minutes, then drizzle half of the sauce over the cooled cake. Serve the rest of the sauce on the side.

PEPPERMINT SWEETS FOR PRIM

Katniss buys peppermints for Prim before returning home to the waiting Peacekeepers. Peppermint candies are usually bought for and by kids and, here, seem to represent innocence — something Katniss desperately needs to prove.
(*Catching Fire*, Chapter 11)

Yields 36–50 Candies

¾ cup condensed milk

1 teaspoon vanilla extract

2 teaspoons peppermint extract

4 cups confectioners' sugar

4 cups semisweet chocolate chips

2 teaspoons shortening

Tips from Your Sponsor

If your dough is a tad crumbly, try rolling it with your hands just slightly moistened. Also, try sticking a thin chopstick or fork into the patties before dipping them into the chocolate. For an extra-fun peppermint patty, dye the dough green or red with food coloring for a bite-sized surprise!

1. Line a baking sheet with waxed paper.

2. In a large bowl, combine milk and extracts. Stir in 3½–4 cups confectioners' sugar to form a stiff dough.

3. Turn dough out onto a clean surface sprinkled with confectioners' sugar. Knead in enough remaining sugar to form a dough that is very stiff and not sticky. Shape into ½" balls.

4. Place balls onto prepared baking sheet. Flatten into small patties and let dry 1 hour. Turn over and let dry 1 more hour. Place patties in freezer for 15–30 minutes.

5. Using a double boiler, melt chocolate and shortening. Allow to thoroughly cool, at least 20 minutes. Dip patties into cooled chocolate mixture and place on waxed paper to harden.

ATTENDANT'S CHAI LATTE

There's nothing like a warm drink to soothe the soul, which is exactly why Katniss's attendant makes her a special chai latte (with honey and spices) when all she requested was a warm glass of milk. (*Catching Fire*, Chapter 14)

Yields 1 mug

1 chai tea bag

4 fluid ounces boiling water

3 fluid ounces half-and-half (preferably heated)

1 tablespoon sugar

1 teaspoon honey

1 pinch ground cardamom

1 pinch ground cinnamon

Tips from Your Sponsor

While a traditional chai latte has foam, this recipe allows you to make yourself a restaurant-quality latte without a fancy steamer. Feel free to mix in more or less cinnamon and cardamom depending on your personal preference.

1. Place the tea bag in a large coffee mug. Add boiling water. Steep for 3 minutes, then remove tea bag.

2. Add in half-and-half, sugar, and honey. Garnish with spices.

CHOCOLATE CUSTARD BREAD PUDDING WITH CARAMEL SAUCE

This dessert can be served with a side bowl of cherries, as Katniss enjoys it, or on its own. Either way, this is a must-try for all chocolate lovers.
(*Catching Fire*, Chapter 14)

Yields 12 servings

> Caramel Sauce:

1 ½ cups white sugar

½ cup water

¼ cup light corn syrup

1 tablespoon lemon juice

1 ¼ cups heavy whipping cream

> Pudding:

2 cups whole milk

2 cups heavy whipping cream

1 cup white sugar

8 (1-ounce) squares semisweet chocolate

8 eggs

2 tablespoons vanilla extract

1 pound egg bread, sliced into 1" pieces

1 cup high-quality bittersweet chocolate chips

Tips from Your Sponsor

Keep an eye on the caramel sauce! The sugar-water-cream mixture takes only about 10 minutes to become caramel, and once it does it will quickly harden into a sugar coating on the bottom of your pan unless you remove it from the heat immediately.

1. For pudding: Preheat oven to 350°F. Lightly oil a 13" x 9" x 2" glass baking dish.

2. Combine milk, 2 cups cream, and 1 cup sugar in another large saucepan over medium-high heat. Stir until sugar dissolves and mixture comes to boil. Remove from heat, add chocolate, and stir until smooth.

3. Beat eggs and vanilla in a large bowl to blend. Gradually whisk in chocolate mixture. Add bread cubes and let stand until bread absorbs some of the custard, stirring occasionally, for at least 45 minutes.

4. Transfer mixture to glass baking dish. Sprinkle top with chocolate chips. Cover with foil.

5. Bake at 350°F until set in center, around 45 minutes. Remove and let sit for at least 10 minutes before serving. Serve pudding warm or at room temperature with warm sauce.

6. For sauce: Stir 1½ cups sugar and the water in a large saucepan over medium-high heat until sugar dissolves. Stir in corn syrup and lemon juice. Increase heat and boil without stirring until syrup turns deep amber, swirling pan occasionally.

7. Remove from heat; pour in the 1¼ cups cream (this will cause mixture to bubble). Stir over low heat until caramel is melted and smooth. Increase heat and boil until sauce is reduced to 12/3 cups, stirring often, about 5 minutes. Remove from heat and pour over pudding.

SPIRIT-LIFTING CHOCOLATE FONDUE

The chocolate fondue that Katniss eats in the Capitol acts as a type of comfort food. Hopefully this chocolate fondue recipe raises your spirits as well.
(*Catching Fire*, Chapter 15)

Yields 4–6 servings

2 tablespoons sugar

1 cup heavy cream

1 teaspoon vanilla extract

4 ounces bittersweet chocolate, chopped

4 ounces semisweet chocolate, chopped

2 tablespoons butter

Tips from Your Sponsor

While fruit is the stereotypical dipper for fondue, try dipping pieces of pound cake or pretzels for a saltier sweet dessert!

1. In a microwave-safe bowl, mix together the sugar, cream, vanilla, both chocolates, and butter. Microwave for 1 minute, stir, then microwave for an additional 90 seconds. Remove from microwave and whisk thoroughly, adding more cream if needed to thin out.

2. Transfer fondue to a fondue pot with a flame underneath. Serve with fresh fruit such as strawberries and apples for dipping.

FINNICK AND ANNIE'S WEDDING APPLE CIDER

In the daily dreariness of the day-to-day at District 13, this delicious apple cider served at the exuberant wedding of Finnick and Annie is a highlight for many. The apple can be seen as a symbol of lust and fertility, which makes cider a perfect wedding beverage.
(*Mockingjay*, Chapter 16)

Yields 10 servings

8 cups apple cider

10 cinnamon sticks

½ cup brown sugar

1 tablespoon ground allspice

2 teaspoons cinnamon

½ teaspoon nutmeg

1 teaspoon whole cloves

Tips from Your Sponsor

Is this cider too sugary for your taste buds? Simply reduce the amount of sugar or, for a different type of sweetness, try adding a tablespoon of vanilla extract and ¼ cup of honey instead of the brown sugar!

1. In a large stockpot over medium-high heat, combine apple cider and cinnamon sticks. Stir in sugar, allspice, cinnamon, nutmeg, and cloves. Still stirring, bring cider to boil over high heat.

2. Reduce heat, and keep warm. Serve each cup with a cinnamon stick.

FINNICK AND ANNIE'S WEDDING: YELLOW CAKE WITH CHOCOLATE BUTTERCREAM FROSTING

Not all brides prefer a white wedding cake; some like a bit of variety in their dessert. For that purpose, it's possible to have a layer (or two) of yellow cake with delicious chocolate buttercream frosting.
(*Mockingjay*, Chapter 16)

Yields one 8" layer cake, or 8–10 servings

> Cake:

2 cups cake flour

2 teaspoons baking powder

1 teaspoon kosher salt

1 cup (2 sticks) butter, room temperature

2 cups white sugar

8 egg yolks

2 teaspoons vanilla extract

1 cup whole milk

> Chocolate Buttercream Frosting:

1 cup shortening

2 teaspoons vanilla extract

5 tablespoons milk

5 cups confectioners' sugar

Pinch of kosher salt

¾ cup high-quality cocoa powder

1. Preheat oven to 350°F. Grease two 8" round pans.

2. For cake: In a medium-sized bowl, sift together the flour, baking powder, and salt. Make sure to thoroughly sift to rid the flour of any oversized lumps.

3. In a large bowl, cream together the butter and sugar until light and fluffy, about 3–5 minutes. Beat in the egg yolks one at a time, then stir in the vanilla. Mix in the flour mixture alternately with the milk, starting and ending with the flour, mixing after each addition until just incorporated. Pour batter into pans.

4. Bake in preheated oven for 25–30 minutes, or until top springs back when lightly tapped. Do not overbake! Let cool on wire racks for 15 minutes before turning out onto the racks to completely cool.

5. For frosting: In a medium bowl, cream together shortening, vanilla, and 5 tablespoons milk until just combined. In another bowl, sift together confectioners' sugar, salt, and cocoa powder. Add dry ingredients to shortening mixture, thoroughly mixing and scraping down sides of the bowl as needed. Once ingredients are thoroughly combined, add additional milk if needed to create a thinner consistency before frosting the cake.

6. Once cakes are thoroughly cooled, frost top and sides of the "bottom" layer of the yellow cake. Place an extra heap of frosting on the top of this layer, then place second layer of yellow cake on top. Thoroughly frost entire cake.

Tips from Your Sponsor

The key to a light and fluffy cake can be found in how long you cream the sugar and butter. The longer you cream, the moister your cake. Cream the butter and sugar for a few good minutes for a cake you won't forget.

FINNICK AND ANNIE'S WEDDING: WHITE WEDDING CAKE

While wedding cakes are different for each bride and groom, this moist white cake likely works as the base (or at least one of the layers) of Finnick and Annie's huge, multi-tiered wedding cake. (*Mockingjay*, Chapter 16)

Yields one 9" x 13" x 2" pan or 10" bundt, or 8–10 servings

1 cup (2 sticks) butter, softened

3 cups white sugar

7 eggs

1 tablespoon vanilla extract

1 teaspoon lemon extract

1 teaspoon almond extract

3 cups all-purpose flour

½ teaspoon kosher salt

¼ teaspoon baking powder

¼ teaspoon baking soda

1 cup sour cream

Tips from Your Sponsor

This cake remains incredibly moist for a couple of days, but tastes best when made the night before or morning of the event at which it will be served. This is a dense cake, but delicious nonetheless. Try with Peeta's Buttercream Frosting (this chapter) for an added dose of sweetness.

1. Preheat oven to 325°F. Grease and flour a 9" x 13" x 2" pan (or 10" bundt pan).

2. In a large bowl, cream together the butter and sugar. Beat in the eggs, one at a time, mixing well after each. Stir in the vanilla extract, followed by the lemon and almond extracts.

3. In a separate bowl, thoroughly combine the flour, salt, baking powder, and baking soda. Add dry mixture to the creamed mixture and mix well. Stir in the sour cream. Mix for 2 minutes, or until there are no lumps. Pour batter into prepared pan.

4. Bake in preheated oven for 45–60 minutes, or until a toothpick inserted into the center of the cake comes out clean. Allow to cool completely before removing from pan.

SECRET SANDWICH COOKIES

While hiding out in a Capitol apartment, Katniss and her team eat a box of cookies. The choice showcases the difference between hunting for food in District 12 and hunting for food in the Capitol; in the former, you have to actually kill your food, in the latter, you can just pick up a box of prepackaged goodies. (*Mockingjay*, Chapter 21)

Yields about 18 cookies

> Cookies:

1 cup (2 sticks) butter

1½ cups confectioners' sugar

1 egg

2 teaspoons vanilla extract

2½ cups all-purpose flour

1 teaspoon baking soda

1 teaspoon cream of tartar

> Filling:

2 cups confectioners' sugar

¼ teaspoon salt

2 teaspoons vanilla extract

6 tablespoons half-and-half

Tips from Your Sponsor

For a chocolate version of this cookie, try adding ¾ cup high-quality unsweetened cocoa to the flour mixture.

1. In a large bowl, cream together butter and confectioners' sugar. Beat in egg and vanilla. Mix well.

2. In another bowl, stir together flour, baking soda, and cream of tartar. Blend into the butter mixture. Divide dough into thirds and shape into balls. Cover balls with plastic wrap and chill in fridge for 2–3 hours.

3. Preheat oven to 350°F. Line a cookie sheet with parchment paper.

4. Remove one ball of dough from refrigerator. Roll out dough into desired thickness on a surface lightly dusted with confectioners' sugar. Cut out cookies using your preferred cookie cutter.

5. Place the cookies on the parchment-lined cookie sheet, leaving at least 1" between each one. Repeat process for remaining balls of dough, working with one ball at a time.

6. Bake in preheated oven 7–8 minutes or until lightly browned. Cool completely on wire rack.

7. While the cookies are baking, mix together all the filling ingredients in a medium-sized bowl. Once the cookies have cooled, frost the top of one cookie with filling; top with another cookie to form the cookie sandwich. Serve.

TIGRIS'S FIG COOKIES

Tigris offers Katniss and the rest of her team fig cookies while they sit down to watch the battle unfold in the Capitol. Figs traditionally represent positive change, which unfolds—if only momentarily—on the television screen.
(*Mockingjay*, Chapter 24)

Yields 2 dozen cookies

2 cups white sugar

1 cup shortening

3 eggs

1 ½ tablespoons vanilla extract

Pinch of kosher salt

4 cups all-purpose flour

1 tablespoon plus ½ teaspoon baking powder

1 cup whole milk

2 pounds dried figs

½ whole orange, with peel

1 small apple, cored and peeled

¼ cup slivered almonds

½ pound raisins

½ cup water (optional)

1 ½ teaspoons ground cinnamon

½ cup white sugar

Tips from Your Sponsor

If you're not a fan of shortening, feel free to substitute unsalted butter. However, if you do so, remember to chill the dough in the refrigerator for at least 1 hour before rolling so the butter sets, which will make rolling the dough much easier.

1. To make dough: Cream 2 cups sugar and 1 cup shortening. Add eggs, vanilla, and salt. Blend in flour and baking powder.

2. Using your bare hands, knead dough until elastic and workable. Add the milk and knead for an additional 5 minutes.

3. To make filling: Cut up figs, orange, and apple into small pieces. Then grind together the figs, orange, apple, almonds, and raisins in a food processor. If too dry or thick, try adding ½ cup water. After the fig mixture is ground, sprinkle in the cinnamon and sugar and knead the mixture. It will be sticky.

4. Preheat oven to 350°F.

5. Roll out a quarter of your dough. Put ¼ of fig mixture in a line down the center of your dough. Wrap dough over mixture, sealing fig mixture inside dough. Cut cookies to desired length, using a diagonal cut and making slits in the sides of each cookie.

6. Bake on ungreased cookie sheet for 15 minutes, then allow to cool on sheet for another ten minutes. Serve with coffee.

KATNISS'S FAMILY BOOK OF HERBS

As in the Hunger Games universe where things aren't always what they seem, when you're foraging, something that looks like a plain old weed can actually be filled with enough nutrients to save a life—as Katniss learned in District 12. Here is a list of some of some of the most popular plants that Katniss may have used to show her resilience and her wild nature— and to save her life in the arena. But be careful: If you're not sure something's edible, don't eat it! Remember Peeta with those berries?

Barberries:

The common barberry, not to be confused with the Japanese barberry, is a thorny shrub that grows in hedgerows and edges of fields and forests across much of the northern United States. It's most easily spotted in the spring when clusters of yellow flowers develop. The fruits of the common barberry hang in drooping clusters and ripen in mid-autumn and remain on the branches through the winter. The fruits are edible and can be used to make jelly.

Burdock:

Burdock is a biennial herb in the sunflower family that was brought to America by Europeans, who got it from Asia, where it has always been valued as food. During its first year, it develops a basal rosette of leaves that are large and fuzzy and continues to grow through the winter. This is the time to dig up the roots.

Cattails:

Cattails are common in most wetlands and in late spring the flower buds begin to develop. You will notice first a slight swelling at the top of a central stalk. Feel with your fingers to determine if it is mature enough to harvest. If so, pull the top leaves back to reveal the greenish flower spikes, which are edible. As the flower buds mature, the male flower—the one on the top—begins to turn yellow. When you tap the spike and see the pollen being dispersed, you know it is ready to collect. Put a plastic bag around the spike and strip the pollen from the stalk. The pollen can then be added to cornmeal or flower for bread. Once it has turned brown, it's past its peak. Eventually the male flowers dry up and drop off, leaving only the female spike.

Chickweed:

Chickweed is an annual that germinates in the fall and grows through the winter. Look for the patches of green in your lawn to locate it. The young plants have slender, sprawling stems with paired leaves that are small, less than one inch long. The tops can be trimmed off until the spring when it finally blooms and goes to seed. Chickweed can be eaten raw or added to salads and herb spreads.

Chicory:

When chicory is young, the basal leaves look very much like a dandelion with deep lobes on some plants and slightly lobed on others, but when it blooms chicory produces beautiful blue flowers. It sends up a stiff flower stalk that produces blue rays that are square at the top with fringes. By midday the flowers have closed up and will be replaced with new flowers the next day. Chicory is a perennial, so once you have located it you can return in the fall and winter to dig up the white, fleshy taproots.

Chokeberries:

Chokeberries are small trees in the eastern United States. There is a red and a black chokeberry. Red chokeberry is common along waterways and in low, wet areas. The fruits turn bright red when ripe in late fall and remain through the winter. The fruits of the black chokeberry are black. The fruits are rather dry and get caught in the throat when eaten raw, giving them the name chokeberry.

Corn Salad:

Corn salad is a low-growing annual herb in the valerian family that waits until after the weather has cooled off to germinate. It often grows in the shade of other plants along the edges of ditches, canals, or damp areas throughout the winter. The basal leaves are small with smooth margins and rounded tips. As soon as the weather starts to get warm, a flower stalk arises with small, white or pale blue flowers in flat-topped clusters surrounded by leafy bracts. The young leaves can be eaten raw and added to salads.

Dandelions:

Dandelions start blooming early, with flower heads appearing randomly in lawns. This is the time to start looking for the buds located in the center of the rosette. Flower buds and flowers are edible. But the best flowers are when you see a profusion of yellow flower heads covering the lawns, growing out of the sidewalks, or popping up in landscaped gardens. These are the sweetest. As the season progresses, the flowers tend to get bitter as do the leaves.

Duck Potatoes:

Also referred to as arrowheads or wapato, duck potatoes are distributed throughout the United States. Not all species have arrowhead-shaped leaves. Some have linear or lance-shaped leaves that emerge from the roots in shallow water. The flower stalk arises from the same root system with no apparent leaves. Flowers with three white petals grow in whorls of three on the stalk and are followed by a greenish ball also in whorls of three. Roots extend out from the base of the plant, sometimes up to two feet, with tubers that develop on the ends. The tubers look and taste very much like potatoes and can be steamed or fried as you would potatoes.

Elder:

Elder is a native shrub with representatives throughout the United States. The most common one in the eastern United States is common elder. Another elder, the red-berried elder, is considered poisonous so check before you eat. Common elder grows along ditches, stream banks, hedgerows, and edges of swamps and blooms in the later part of spring with an abundance of large, white, flat-topped clusters of flowers. Finding elder is easy. The large, white flowers can be spotted from the car while driving down the road. Once the flower heads have filled out, use pruning scissors to snip off the tops. Elder flowers are edible, either dipped in batter and fried or infused in water for a tea. They can also be dried and used later to make tea.

Evening Primrose:

Evening primrose is a biennial that comes up from seed in late summer or early fall and forms a basal rosette of leaves that are often speckled with red spots and remain green through the winter. A white, starchy taproot develops underground and can be dug anytime through the winter as long as the ground is not frozen. Roots can be used as a cooked vegetable or with other vegetables.

Groundnuts:

Groundnuts are members of the pea family that have bean-like vines with compound leaves. Look for them along the sunny edges of waterways, climbing up trees and shrubs along the banks. In midsummer they develop clusters of maroon-colored blossoms that are followed by pods containing edible beans that look and taste like garden peas.

Heal-all:

Found growing along damp, woodland trails year round, heal-all has small, almost triangular leaves that develop through the winter. The surfaces of the leaves have small bumps that can be felt when you rub your fingers across them. In the spring a flower stalk develops. The stem leaves are paired, oval-shaped, and are larger than the basal leaves. The purple, snapdragon-like flowers are about one-half inch long and form a dense spike at the top of the stem. After the plant has bloomed, the seed stalk will dry on the plant, making it easy to identify in the fall and winter.

Horse Balm and Bee Balm:

Horse balm and bee balm are members of the mint family that bloom in late summer with a scent that resembles thyme. Horse balm has yellowish, purple-dotted flowers that grow in whorls in the upper leaf axils with white or pale purple bracts at their base. It grows in dry, sandy soil along the coastal plain and on the prairies of the Midwest. Bee balm has bright red, tubular flowers and grows in moist soil along streams.

Life Everlasting:

Life everlasting blooms later in the summer and looks like a lot of other plants blooming at that time. The scent is the trademark. It's unlike any other. The leaves are several inches long and feel woolly to the touch with whitish hairs underneath. The flowers are white, cotton-like and fragrant, as are the leaves. It grows in dry clearings, fields, and edges of woods throughout the eastern United States.

Lilies:

Familiar members of the lily family include several species of wild onions and garlic, sometimes collectively referred to as onion grass because of their grass-like leaves and strong onion scent. The emerging young leaves are edible raw or added to cooked vegetables or soups. The bulbs can be used as a substitute for onions and garlic.

Mesquite:

In the southwest is the mesquite, a small tree in the pea family that grows along streams and in areas where the water table is relatively high, from southern Kansas to southeastern California. Look for the spikes of greenish-yellow flowers in the early spring, followed by pods that become brittle and brown when fully ripe, usually in the fall. Gather the pods when they are mature and make a flour by grinding the pods to make into cakes or mush. The seeds are hard and should be discarded.

Milkweed:

Milkweed is a perennial and in the spring sends up new shoots that are edible. Flower buds begin developing in midsummer and soon open into fragrant, pinkish-colored flowers. A pod-like fruit with a rough surface soon follows. Flower buds, flowers, and young pods are all edible after preparing by boiling for one minute, pouring the water off, and boiling a second time, after which you can strain and use as a cooked vegetable. All parts of the milkweed are poisonous when raw so be careful.

Mulberries:

Mulberries are medium-sized trees with fruits that look like blackberries. All are edible but some have more flavor than others. White mulberries are mostly bland tasting while red or black berries are sweet.

Mustards:

Members of the mustard family have flower buds that look like miniature versions of cultivated broccoli. When the flower buds open, the four petals form a cross, giving them the generic name of crucifers. The colors vary from white and yellow to pink and purple. All mustards are edible and have a spicy odor and taste, some more than others. Almost all of them are palatable in some form. Flower buds and flowers are edible, either raw or cooked.

Nettles:

Stinging nettle has square stems that are covered with stinging hairs. Leaves are opposite and have toothed margins, coming to a point at the tip. They also have spines that are like miniature hypodermic needles that inject several chemicals, including histamine, that cause the stinging sensation. Nettles can be safely eaten after boiling them in water for two minutes.

Nutgrass:

Nutgrass is recognized by its umbrella-like flower head with grass-like leaves radiating out from under the flowering rays. Flower stalks have edges, a triangular stem, as is characteristic of many of the sedges. The tubers are somewhat nutty tasting and can be dug any time the ground is not frozen. They can be eaten raw, roasted, or cooked as a vegetable.

Oxeye Daisy:

Oxeye daisy flowers look like large chamomile flowers and taste very similar in a tea. The dark green leaves with deep lobes form a rosette of basal leaves and continue up the flower stalk, getting smaller as they near the top where the large, white flower, up to two inches wide, is located. The petals are white with a yellow center that has a depression in the middle. They can be found in fields, pastures, and roadsides.

Patridgeberry:

Partridgeberry is a trailing, evergreen vine in the bedstraw family. The woody stems have paired, roundish leaves about a half-inch long and often with white veins. White, tubular flowers with four petals appear in June and July, covering the forest floor with a white carpet. Partridgeberries are edible and ripen in the late fall, often remaining on the vine through the winter. Although they are lacking in taste, they make a colorful addition to fruit salads and make a pleasant nibble while hiking in the woods.

Pokeweed:

Pokeweed is a tall, perennial herb with oval-shaped leaves and a thick stem that turns red as summer progresses. Fruits develop in late summer or early fall and turn purplish-black. Poke must be cooked before eating.

Purslane:

Purslane is a low-growing, succulent herb that waits until after the last frost to emerge, which is usually late spring. Leaves are rounded at the top and may be either alternate or opposite. These can be trimmed and the plant will continue to grow and sprawl out in different directions. The trimmings can be added raw to salads, soups, or as a cooked green. Small, yellow flowers appear in midsummer followed by black seeds. Leaves, stems, flowers, and seeds are all edible.

Rock Tripe:

Rock tripe is a foliose lichen that grows on rocks in open woods from the arctic south to the northern United States and in the mountains south to Georgia. The top surface is gray to olive-brown while the underside is black. It is attached near the center and expands outward very slowly, forming a circular shape as it grows. After a rain, while it is wet, it feels leathery and smooth. As it dries, it becomes brittle. Rock tripe can be gathered by tearing off pieces, leaving the center attached so it will continue to grow. Rock tripe is edible and can be added to soups.

Serviceberries:

Serviceberries are one of the first trees to bloom in the understory of the forest in the spring before the leaves have come out. They are easily spotted at that time of the year when the tree is covered with white flowers. Members of the rose family, the flowers have five petals and are about an inch wide. About a month after the tree has bloomed, the fruits begin to ripen. They are best when they turn a deep red or purplish color. The fruits are mildly juicy and have a slight, almond-like flavor.

Spicebush:

Spicebush is a shrub that grows in shady areas, sometimes bordering streams, where the soil is moist. The leaves are oval and simple, so simple they are often overlooked. In the early spring it produces small, yellow flowers on the branches. The twigs are distinctive with a spicy aroma when scratched and sniffed. This is the part used to make tea.

Strawberries:

Wild strawberries look like strawberries, except they are much smaller. What they lack in size they make up for in taste. They are usually found in light areas within the forest or along its edges. A member of the rose family, strawberries have flowers with five white petals in the early spring.

Sweet Birch:

Sweet birch grows in cool, moist upland forests with smooth, dark brown bark. Leaves are doubly-toothed and come to a sharp point at the tip. The cone-like fruit is small and brown and contains two-winged nutlets. The twigs and branches of sweet birch, when scratched or broken, smell like wintergreen and can be made into a tea.

Sweet Goldenrod:

This is a goldenrod that can be distinguished from all other goldenrods by its taste, which is a sweet, anise-like flavor. The leaves are from 1–4" long and narrow, with smooth edges. About midsummer the yellow clusters of flowers appear along one side of arching branches. Look for it in dry fields and open woods in the eastern United States.

Thistle:

Thistles are biennials in the sunflower family. Fleshy roots of some species are edible, although somewhat bitter. Early in the spring of the second year, a flower stalk develops. The best time to harvest it is just before the flower bud opens. It can be eaten raw as a celery substitute or cooked as a vegetable.

Toyon Berries:

The toyon berry is in the rose family and is an evergreen shrub or small tree that is limited in its range to lower elevations from northern to southern California. It blooms in the summer with white flowers followed by the fruit which look like little apples and ripen in the winter. The berries can be eaten raw but can also be dried and ground into flour, steeped in hot water for tea, or made into pies or jellies.

Violets:

Violets are familiar weeds for most people. They come up in lawns, in the forest, along stream banks, and just about every place where people go. Some have blue flowers, others have white, and one has yellow—this is the one you don't eat.

Violet flowers taste mildly sweet. They can be eaten raw, infused in water for a flower tea or candied and made into jams, jellies, and syrups.

Wintergreen:

Wintergreen is in the heath family, along with blueberries and cranberries. It is a low-lying, evergreen herb that grows in acid woodlands from Newfoundland to Manitoba and south to Georgia and Alabama. It spreads on the forest floor with horizontal rhizomes just beneath the surface. The leaves contain compounds that add a wintergreen flavor to tea. Look for the little black, resinous dots under the leaves for positive identification.

Yampa:

Yampa is one of eight species and a member of the carrot family that is found throughout the west. Like other members of the carrot family, it has flat-topped clusters of small, white flowers. The narrow leaves look like stems and arise from clusters of edible roots. The time to gather them is in the fall after the plant has gone to seed. The roots should be washed and peeled before using as a cooked vegetable. They can also be dried and ground as a flour.

Yucca:

Yucca is in the agave family and is easily recognized by its sharp-pointed, dagger-like leaves that form a rosette. In the late spring and early summer, a flower stalk rises from the center and produces large, white, bell-shaped flowers at the top. The young flower stalks of yucca are edible when they're about a foot tall. They resemble asparagus at this stage. Some taste better than others, even when growing side by side. Do the taste test before including them in a recipe. Yucca flowers are also edible. The reproductive parts in the center are bitter and should be removed. Flowers can be eaten raw or cooked with other vegetables.

ACKNOWLEDGMENTS

Completing an acknowledgment section is nearly as impossible as winning the Hunger Games. After all, I'll inevitably forget to thank someone who deserves thanking. So let me begin this long note of thanks with a note of apology: If I forget to mention you, I apologize, and by the time you are reading this I've realized your name isn't in this list and feel terrible. Thus, to all my friends, family, coworkers past and present—thank you.

Special thanks to agent extraordinaire Danielle Chiotti of Upstart Crow Literary for making this possible and helping me come to terms with the importance of high-quality chocolate. A hug to Andrea Hakanson, Katie Corcoran Lytle, and all the folks at Adams Media who helped put this cookbook together.

Love and thanks to my grandmother Marlene Boles for the baking genes, my mother Jenine for the unending love and encouragement, my father for the support both physical and mental, and my brother for the pats on the back.

Thanks to all my friends, near or far—I love you all dearly. Special thanks goes to Keagan Buchanan, the best best friend a girl could have, and his entire family for their love, encouragement, and for hosting the many dinner parties where I witnessed true culinary artistry. Intense gratitude to Spam Weishoff for keeping me sane and loving me no matter what, to Katie Weishoff for the great hugs and for being one of my original readers, and to my other reader, Dan, for the practical (and blunt) advice. Continued appreciation to everyone in the EEP crowd for helping me grow up while remaining young-spirited. A heartfelt hug to Vince Mateus.

Thank you Estella Soto, Kevin Biggers, Liza Kaplan, Ernie Duque, Sarah LaBrie, Joel Smith, and all the members of writing group. Without your wisdom I'd be an idiot with long sentences and poor grammar. Thank you Erin McCulloch, who has supported me no matter where I move or what I do. Erin, you will one day take over the world and I hope you'll let me sit next to you. Thanks to Alice and Merry Kahn, for being not only fellow cat lovers but two of the original supporters of this cookbook. Love to Ollie Brooks, who is ten times the chef I will ever be, and to Mary Rotzien and Oakley Gillett for all the great recipe links and tips. Unending gratitude to Aimee Bender and Ron Carlson for the years of wisdom and advice. Thanks to Mr. Vaughn for telling me in ninth grade he'd shoot me if I became anything other than a writer.

Special appreciation goes to everyone at Sound Lounge and RadioFace, who patiently put up with my many baking mistakes and subsequent discoveries. Let us not forget Suzanne Collins. Thank you for writing *The Hunger Games* trilogy in the first place. Your talent for storytelling still astounds me.

Last but certainly not least, a large thank you to Nicholas Stefanovich. I love you. Thank you for making sure I woke up early to work on this. Thank you for loving me. You are the wisest—and wittiest—man I know.

INDEX

ABOUT THE AUTHOR

Emily Ansara Baines is a writer who has worked as a professional baker and caterer throughout the East Coast, most recently New York City. When Emily isn't busy writing, baking, or trying to learn how to dance, she's reading her favorite series, The Hunger Games trilogy, in hopes of one day becoming as self-reliant and cool as Katniss. Emily currently lives in Los Angeles, California.